Industry Response To "Pull"

"'PULL' reads like a fast paced novel and teaches lessons with immediate results which continue to produce exponentially through the years."

— George F. Bauer, *Former President/CEO of the Miss America Organization*

"We hired Keith Chambers when we first started *Stagg Foods* in 1972. When we sold *Stagg* in 1997 to Hormel, he remained our 'hired gun.'"

— Bo Hirsch, *President, Stagg Foods 1980—1995*

"'PULL' makes sense, and it works."

— Henry Haskell, *Owner, Square-H Brands, Inc.*

"Keith focuses on what motivates the customer at the point of impact. He breaks marketing execution down into a communications framework that anyone can understand and use."

— Stephen Bohnet, *Sr. Vice President, Ipsos Vantis Research*

"Keith's approach to developing breakthrough offerings is truly unique and innovative, yet seems so painfully obvious once you see it in 'PULL'."

— Amy Abdallah, *President Research, Inside Out, Chicago*

PULL

Keith Chambers

All Polimedia titles, imprints, and distributed lines are available at special quantity discounts for bulk purchases for sales promotion, premiums, fund-raising, educational, or institutional use.

2 3 4 5 6 7 8 9 10

Published by Polimedia Publishers
© 2009 Keith Chambers

ISBN-10: 0-9768617-7-1
ISBN-13: 978--0-9768617-7-5
Printed in China by Global PSD

Special book excerpts or customized printings can also be created to fit specific needs. For details, write or contact the office of Polimedia Publishing at:

Polimedia Publishers
100 S. Sunrise Way #A670, Palm Springs, CA 92262
info@polimediaent.com
www.polimediaent.com

I would like to acknowledge my two best friends without whose support and inspiration this book would not have been possible.
Branden Scott Chambers and Eric David Chambers

TABLE OF CONTENTS

PREFACE i

1 The Early Years 1

2 Evolution of a Marketing Master 7
    The First Turning Point 9
    The Second Turning Point.. 11
    Ownership is Fickle.. 14

3 Why I'm Giving Away the Keys 17
    The Pitch 17
    The Activist 19
    The Pacifist.. 20
    The Indifferent... 22
    The Myth 24
    This is the Motivational Section.................................... 25

4 The Marketing Objective 27
    Two Critical Functions 27
    The Two Components of a Successful Selling Proposition 27
    Your Selling Proposition 28
    The Power of the Selling Proposition....................... 30
    Your Impact Point... 32
    Multiple Impact Points 34
    Being Aggressive... 38

5 The Creative Side — Positioning and Repositioning 41

New Product and Service Development.................................. 41
The Inflated Value of Ideas.. 42
Product and Service Positioning... 44
100% Positioning 48
Product and Service Repositioning 50

6 A Few Critical Insights 53

What's Next?.. 53
Being Active is Critical 57
A Little Work Now 58
A Bit of Advice.. 60
Context and Agreement... 62
Adapting to the Moment.. 63

7 The Remarkability Paradigm 67

What Lies Ahead? 67
The Operating State.. 68
The Paradigm Framework 70
Product/Service vs. Selling Proposition 74
The Importance of Triggers... 75
Dealing with "Pull" 76
The Power of Character.. 78
The Truing Principle... 81

8 More on Remarkability.................................... 85

Remarkability Before the Paradigm 85
The Origin of Remarkability 85
Character and Loyalty 87
Character and Profits 89
Category Evolution and Natural Selection............................. 90

9 The Communications Model **91**

Naming Possibilities 93
The Generic Descriptor 95
The Brand 98
The Sub-Brand 105
Segments 107
The Benefit 109
  • Looking a Little Further 114
  • Empowering Your Benefit 117
Attributes 117
  • Negative Attributes 124
  • Relevant to You 126
The Tag Line 127
The Endorsement 130
The Key Graphic 131
The Impact 134
The Product Configuration 136
The Container Configuration 137
The Product Presentation 142
The Delivery System 144
The Graphic Presentation 147
Being Attractive—People vs. Products 155

10 Pursuing Remarkability **157**

Working with the Target 157
Working with Research 161
Do It Yourself 162
The Two Types of Research 162

11 Walk the Walk **165**

12 Creative Preparation 171

Creating "What's Next?" 171
Tattoos are "Cool" 172
Success Is Labor Intensive 173
I Learned Rigor 174
When Hope Replaces Rigor 174
Great References 177
Backgrounding 177

13 Applying This to Your Business 179

Scope 180
The Procedure—Part I 181
The Procedure—Part II 183
The Process 184
   • Generic Descriptor 184
   • Brand or Sub-Brand 186
   • Segments 189
   • Benefit 191
   • Attributes 192
   • Tag Line 194
   • Endorsements 195
   • Key Graphic 197
   • Product or Service Configuration 198
   • Container Configuration 199
   • Product Presentation 200
   • Delivery System 202
Making Critical Choices 203
The Conservative Choice 204
Graphic Presentation 206
Impact 208

Reference Materials 211

Glossary 218

Index 220

About the Author 223

"There is a force in the marketing universe that compels humans to take anything that occurs as extraordinary and quickly make it ordinary. I call it 'pull'. 'Pull' is ever present, relentless, and if you are not keenly aware of its effect, it is most likely costing you a great deal of money."

— Keith A. Chambers

PREFACE

We humans have a natural tendency to accumulate stuff. As we interact with each other, we tend to exchange our stuff. During this process, we strive to amass more stuff than our fellow humans. Conversely, it is not at all human nature to freely give our stuff to others. This unrelenting process literally guarantees the ongoing existence of what many refer to as free enterprise. Over time, I have come to realize that our global society is literally powered by it. If this is true, then free enterprise is fundamental to life on this planet and must be dealt with by all of us. You and I have no say in the matter of dealing with free enterprise.

Our relationship with free enterprise is identical to that of our relationship with gravity—our lives are controlled by the fundamental laws of both, yet we operate as if we are unaffected by either. We ignore their existence. This is true in spite of the fact that we have invented marketing to deal with it. Marketing is essentially the study of free enterprise. Unlocking the true nature of free enterprise and creating a remarkable set of marketing tools to deal with it, is exactly what this book is about. With these tools you will have the opportunity to develop an extraordinary sales message for your product or service, and your competition—not having that advantage—will be devastated.

The Early Years
Chapter One

I got my first job at the age nine. My parents had moved my brother and me to a house across the street from a golf course in Midwestern Ohio. On weekends, when the course got crowded, I would take up a watching post in one of the two trees in my front yard. The tree I chose was tall and thin and swayed easily, even in a mild breeze. That tree defined the moment when I became a pilot. The U.S. Air Force would say it was 18 years later when I entered flight training at Williams Air Force Base outside of Phoenix, but that was simply where I learned to fly; I became a pilot in that tree. I'll refer to that later, so back to the golf course for now. Little did I know just how much other good stuff I would discover that year.

I was fascinated with how well-groomed all of that open space was and couldn't wait to explore it. Once I discovered how to cruise the fairways and creeks in the early morning and late afternoon when few golfers were around, the course became my private domain.

It wasn't long before my older brother Jon started making money shagging golf balls and working as a caddy. The whole idea of making money was new to me. My dad made money, of course, but the concept escaped me until my 11-year-old brother, of all people, opened my eyes. I was jealous of him because I was too young and too small to caddy, and felt left out. My brother was big enough to caddy which meant that he could buy soda and candy bars and all I could do was beg. Sometimes he would share a swig or a bite but seldom a whole bottle or bar. I had no money and somehow knew, even at that age, that I needed to earn some. My breakthrough was just ahead.

Early one morning, before the golfers showed up, I was cruising the empty course when I spotted an older kid sitting on the creek bank. He was doubled over doing something to his foot. I was sure he had been wading as his jeans were rolled up above his knees, and figured he had cut himself. We used to throw our pop bottles into the creek and they would sometimes break and sink down into the muck.

The thick black muck was about a foot deep in the middle of the creek. It smelled awful when you dredged it up, and seemed to suck you down when you walked in it. As I got closer, a new reality set in. The kid had not cut his foot but was instead burning off a leech that had hooked itself there. I'd never seen that before and it sent a shiver down my back. This kid, treating it like it was no big deal, impressed me with his bravery. Watching him carefully, I learned there was a definite technique for getting rid of a bloodsucker—you need to put the match flame directly to its tail end or it won't let go. If you try to yank a leech off, it will leave its tiny head behind in your skin causing an infection; it was creepy just thinking about it.

I also noticed that the kid's pockets were full of golf balls that he had been gathering from the creek. He showed them to me and boastfully estimated their value. He had over $3 worth based upon what he thought the golfers would pay. He also had a small pile of balls that were badly discolored. Some looked like the covers were half melted away. He explained that he was look-ing for balls that had been hit into the creek within the last two days. They would be sitting under the water but still on top of the muck. The discolored balls in his pile had been in the water more than a couple days, and had sunk deep down where they were literally being eaten by the muck.

I decided to hang around with him to see how he would convert his find into cash. As it turned out, he did it by cleverly positioning himself on the fifth tee, out of sight of the pro shop, where he patiently waited for golfers to come by. It didn't take long; in the time it took for three foursomes to play through, he sold every ball. He made $2.25—all profit. Looking back, I realize this is still the only business I know of that has no overhead. At least it seemed so at the time. I was fascinated by what he had accomplished and could not stop thinking about it.

That experience proved to be the key to my first career move. I could do this, I told myself, no matter how small or how young I was. I started first thing the next morning. They called kids like us "ball hounds" and there weren't very many of us. You might think every kid would do it for the easy money, but most couldn't deal with the leeches. Owing to our superior courage, we "ball hounds" were considered elite by the other ordinary kids, and I liked that. Elite and only nine years old!

Suddenly I was in business. Find them, and sell them—WOW, easy! There were now plenty of pop and candy bars for me. There were even days when my brother did not get to caddy and I made more money than he did. That always put a smile on my face because all the caddies ever talked about at the end of the day was how much money they had made. It occurs to me now that in the ensuing years nothing, absolutely nothing, has changed. Not even the leeches.

When my mom discovered I was carrying matches, she was sure I was smoking cigarettes. She knew that all the caddies smoked, which they did, except for me and my brother. Both of our parents smoked like crazy, but Jon and I never did. After telling my mom what the matches were really for—removing leeches—I had to convince her that I rarely needed them; the possibility of her little boy being attacked by leeches repulsed her more than the possibility of me smoking. She would sit me down and run through all the various diseases I could contract from a leech. Looking back, I'm sure she was exaggerating, but it certainly put a damper on my enthusiasm for my business. She agreed to let me continue but only if I promised to tell her every time I had to burn off a leech. Of course I never did tell her, since that would have ended my career for sure.

Then, just as my career was really taking off, things took a completely unexpected turn that I never would have envisioned. My mom stepped into the middle of my enterprise, as well as my brother's, and altered the free enterprise dynamic forever. My mom, thinking it very resourceful of my brother and I to have found a way to generate income, took it upon herself to find what she characterized as a "good use" for the money. Until that moment, I had never considered the need for a "good use" for money; to me, all uses, if they made me happy, were pretty good (in fact, it wasn't until I had kids of my own that I really understood this "good use" thing).

My mom, in her wisdom, had decided that my brother and I would put our money aside in order to buy our back-to-school clothes at the end of summer. Suddenly, things were just not the same. What to me had been pure fun and excitement now became work; I now had a job. A job, and I was only nine years old. Damn! (Oh yeah, if you were a caddy in those days, you quickly developed a colorful vocabulary to go with the cigarettes; luckily I avoided the cigarettes, but I carry the vocabulary to this day.)

Fortunately, it was only a matter of weeks before my attitude towards earning money shifted again. I happened to overhear my dad telling one of our neighbors that I was making money, and I was struck by the tone of his voice—Dad was bragging. A few days later he acknowledged my accomplishment to me directly, and my mom started doing it as well. What had begun as pure fun, then morphed into just work, had now turned into a source of pride. At nine I was hooked on success. Determined to move up and improve my lot, I swore that I'd eventually become a caddy just like my brother.

After a few more summers had come and gone, I came to realize that money in our home was not plentiful and that my brother and I were, in a small way, helping to subsidize our family's expenses. I always kept that fact away from my friends; I found the need to work for my school clothes embarrassing. Since I was the only kid I knew who had to do that, it made me feel like we were poor. I spent a lot of time trying to prove otherwise, another behavioral trait I still carry today.

A few years later, the concept of free enterprise was formally introduced to me in a seventh-grade textbook. At the time, it seemed like a pretty "cool" concept. I could understand that power and respect came along with earning one's own money. It seemed like the more money you had, the more power and respect you got. I decided I would be rich when I grew up—really rich.

By that time I was working as a caddy and admiring the rich businessmen I worked for. They had an air of independence and power that was missing in all the working class adults that I knew. In particular, I remember Mr. Popkin. He was in his 50s and not particularly attractive, but had a strong aura of confidence and a hot-looking wife in her 30s—I was quite impressed with both. I fantasized that some day I'd be even richer than Mr. Popkin and have an even more beautiful wife...maybe even a movie star. Of course I knew it was all a fantasy and didn't have a clue how to turn it into reality. I now realize that all the success that Mr. Popkin and his buddies enjoyed was based upon their ability to sell themselves and their ideas to the people who mattered. That realization is the inspiration behind this book: how each and every one of us can be effective and, in turn, successful in a business environment.

And, what is that business environment like? That seventh-grade text book clearly and logically explained its fundamentals, but I have since discovered that the book fell short in one critical aspect—it failed to mention that free enterprise is basically an all-out economic war.

While that may seem exaggerated, it is deadly accurate. If you don't believe me, you will likely become a casualty very soon—and there are lots of casualties. There are good guys and bad guys in this war, and sometimes the good guys win, but not always. Sometimes the bad guys go to jail, but mostly not. Sometimes whole brands or businesses are destroyed or simply disappear. Refugees become consultants until they find a new cause and turn into soldiers again. The good news for you is that you are no longer alone; with this book, you now have me at your side as a "hired gun". When it comes to your business, your life just got a whole lot better.

As for me, well, I grew up and became that "hired gun". A mercenary, if you will. I have personally developed the weapons and will show you exactly how to use them just as I do for my own clients. That is what this book is about. It's about winning the battles, and in turn winning the economic war. Creating success. It's about you creating your own economic success. It's no accident that professional marketers refer to their "prey" as "target consumers", for they are targets and treated so in every respect. I recommend you too, think of them in that way from now on.

Now, it's true that the bulk of my experience has been with the "big boys"— big players in Corporate America. What I have done here, is transform my experience into a format perfectly suited to any business, no matter its size, small, medium or large. After all, the weapons are exactly the same.

I can say with certainty that right now, you are in the process of selling something. How do I know? Because you, me and every other human on this planet are all selling our butts off 24/7. We do it so frequently and subtly that we're often completely unaware of whether we're doing it well or poorly. How effective you are in all aspects of your life absolutely depends on your awareness of just how often you are involved in selling a winning proposition. So stay tuned—your level of awareness is about to change.

As you read Chapter Two, I want you to think about your own relationship with free enterprise. What was the nature of your first encounter with it? What is your opinion of it as an economic system? How do you relate to it as a human? Do you play freely within it or are you at the effect of it? I will further characterize it in a very realistic way that will have you view it differently. Your awareness of it will become your way of being and you will become significantly more effective than ever before.

Evolution of
a Marketing Master
Chapter Two

Like it or not, free enterprise is now the most pervasive economic structure in the world. It is so persistent that it has become transparent. Transparent much in the same way that water is transparent to fish. Ask any fish and you will discover that they do not know they are in water. We humans are immersed too. We are literally swimming in free enterprise and yet we don't acknowledge its existence or the effect it has on our lives. We simply swim and swim and swim. We began swimming at a very early age without intention. It happened naturally and without effort because we were surrounded by it. We have all been forced into the same pool with only some say about which lane we are allowed to swim in.

Free enterprise is a "game", a competition into which all of us have been thrown with little warning and even less training, and we are all expected to win. Furthermore, it is a mandatory game in that we must play just like fish must swim. You and I have absolutely no say in the matter of free enterprise. Even if you escape to a commune or get a shopping cart and take to the streets, you will soon discover that free enterprise is alive and well, and you must swim there too.

Over time I have noticed that somehow we have all learned to swim. It was in fact fairly easy for most of us, as we humans seem to come by it naturally. This book assumes that you are all accomplished swimmers and therefore what lies ahead is far more than swimming lessons. By now you may have noticed that learning to swim is merely learning to survive. If so, you have just taken the first step toward taking control of your business and, in turn, your life.

Myself, I am an accomplished surfer and I am going to share with you exactly how to surf the universe of free enterprise irrespective of your level of involvement. Surfing takes place on top of the water, where your awareness of the water's existence is profound and where your awareness is the direct access to creating success.

Over the past three decades, I estimate that I have received more than 500 assignments from consumer goods and services companies asking that I create their vital marketing communications. Being entrusted so often with this responsibility has had a profound effect on my life.

In the early days, my goal was simply to produce results that were better than my competition. I soon discovered that this was incredibly easy to do. As it turned out, the rate of marketing success in the consumer goods and services industry was, to put it bluntly, lousy. Even today, the success rate remains extremely low; marketers continue to throw new product and service concepts into research knowing that only about one in 30 will score well enough to continue developing, and only one in 300 will get launched into the market. Their bigger problem is that they can't find 30 to throw into the research. It seems failure is so prevalent in the industry that a high level of it has become acceptable.

I also discovered early on that I could not tolerate anywhere near such a level of failure in my life, whether it was acceptable or not. From the very beginning, I have taken failure personally and that has not changed; if anything, my commitment to success has only gotten stronger. I knew from the start that if I was going to continue in this business I would have to develop a methodology that could be relied upon to consistently produce success.

My strategy for learning how to create success was simple; I began monitoring it wherever I could find it. Given my personal involvement in so many projects, I was afforded the opportunity to observe many successes as well as failures, firsthand. I was exposed to the launch of a new business about every three to four weeks.

As I observed, month after month, I was able to identify things that routinely worked. As time passed, I made notes and found I had trouble keeping them organized or even finding them. You see, the insights come whenever they feel like it. More often than not they come to me in the night or early in the morning when I am at home. I had notes everywhere and was sure I was losing many of them. One night I woke up and was so anxious to record my thought, I wrote it on a paper plate that was handy.

I soon noticed how incredibly easy that note was to keep track of and, you guessed it, paper plates have been my medium for ground-breaking thoughts since that night. There came a day when those plates were used to organize all of my observations on my living room floor. That day was when I discovered what we generally refer to as the remarkability paradigm. It emerged and ultimately proved to be the secret to marketing success. That paradigm forms the basis of this book and is all that is required for you too, to create success for yourself. When it comes to creating success, it is accurate to assume that on that day I literally "cracked the code" that I am now sharing it with you. These days I get laughed at a lot for my paper plates, but out of sheer respect, am not likely to let go of the habit.

The First Turning Point

It occurred to me that all businesses experience periodic pivotal turning points. That point is when a significant change in the way we conduct our business results in a significant change in direction. Such turning points typically cause business to turn severely up or down. Any change in the middle typically goes unnoticed by the target consumer. When we are in the midst of these turning points, we become so consumed by dealing with the change that its long-term significance may go unnoticed, only becoming apparent with the passage of time. These changes become historical milestones that only we in the business are aware of. Irrespective of what they look like as we encounter them, even if they seem completely negative, I believe they all represent opportunities. How well we respond to these chances is a major factor in the amount of success we enjoy.

If you are just beginning your career, these milestones most likely lie ahead. If you are well into it, you are already aware of their existence. In either case, by sharing my own experiences I will help you acknowledge those turning points that have already had their effect, and open your eyes to those yet to come.

There have been two major turning points in my career. The first came in 1988 when San Francisco-based Sega of America asked us to develop a package design image for its new high-powered home video game platform. This new system would be twice as powerful as the market leader Nintendo. Sega's intention was clear: dethrone Nintendo and take over as the market leader.

To our surprise, they did not have a name for the system and asked if we could develop one. This was our first such assignment. Fortunately, the client never asked for a list of previous naming successes or the gig might have ended right there. They had not yet selected an advertising agency or they would have given the assignment to them.

I remember rushing the job as fast as we could in order to get it settled before the agency came on board. It seemed as if I was the only one who knew how badly the agency would want to create the name. We proceeded with the assignment as if we knew exactly what we were doing and got it done just before the agency selection was announced.

What we created was the brand Sega Genesis, which was launched that year to rave reviews. Even more importantly, Sega Genesis became a $500-million brand in its second year. Our organization became an overnight authority on naming and beyond.

The first thing we discovered in the process of creating a name was that, while the name was important, we needed to communicate a great deal about the product beyond the name if we expected to be successful. From that day forward, package design became an element, albeit a critical one, within the greater task of positioning brands and products for our clients.

For those of you who may not be familiar with the term "positioning", it simply refers to the sales message. Professional marketers think of it in terms of a specific message directed at the consumers they are targeting.

Without any prior intent, but as a result of our success with Sega Genesis, we evolved instantly into a branding and positioning company (the only difference between the two being that positioning is generally thought of as the sales message for one product while branding refers to a group of products). Most likely, you've noticed such unintended evolutions without prior intention showing up in your own life as well.

The Second Turning Point

My second career turning point had far less effect on what services we offer, but a tremendous impact on how we conduct our business. It also had a profound personal impact as well.

By 1999, in addition to positioning and branding, we were well established as a reliable resource for creating new product pipeline concepts. A "new product pipeline" is simply an industry term referring to an inventory of eight or ten new product concepts to launch over a two- or three-year period. By that time we had also developed and perfected the art of positioning and branding. Specifically this means creating the image, including the words and graphics that communicate a product or service to its target consumer. It was at this point in my career that we received a very cool assignment from a San Francisco-based client.

The client had developed a great new product and needed a "killer" positioning effort from us (I use the word "killer" when nothing else will express how powerful and effective our positioning approach needs to be.) To this day I am unable to disclose the brand or the exact nature of the product because I signed a "non-disclosure" agreement I must honor. I can only say it was something that would clean your kitchen floor and make it shine for an unusually long time. We worked closely with the client over the next few weeks perfecting this "killer" image, including the entire sales message on the front of the package. At that point, all of us, including the client, were fully enamored of what we had created. All that was left was a bit of research to confirm what we already knew—that we had done a great job.

The client set up focus groups in Phoenix, Chicago and Philadelphia and asked that I attend the first two in Phoenix. At that time, to be completely honest, I hated research. I have now been working with groups of people for over ten years and have learned one absolute truth. It is that the operating mental state of humans is, "What's wrong here?" If you are like me, your first reaction to this is that it may be true for everyone else but not me. It may take some time for you to buy into that one, but if you watch carefully you will see it is true…that includes you and me as well. It is a generalization but one that you can count on, and your staying aware of it while you are marketing your product or service will serve you well. My experience is that if you gather a small group of people, show them something and ask them, "What do you think about this", you will get almost all negative responses centered on what is wrong with it. You can go further by asking, "What do you like about this?" You will get one or two positive responses, then without hesitation they will begin telling you what is wrong with it. Consider the possibility that the origin of this state of mind is survival in nature, and comes from a time when humans lived in caves and there was in fact always something wrong.

It seemed to me that researchers lived only to perpetuate my assumption that consumers are perpetually looking for what is wrong. At least that was my mind-set going into Phoenix, that all researchers dedicate themselves to disqualifying new concepts. To appease the client, I pretended that I believed it was a great idea to conduct this one final check before committing to the product launch.

While flying over, I remember thinking we might get lucky and pick up a few bits and pieces of feedback that would allow us to improve the concept even more. Truthfully, I suppose I was trying to avoid the thought that we might actually fail. Realistically, I knew we were flying to Phoenix to discover what was wrong with the concept and, frankly, I hated that.

Later that evening, at the Thomas Mall on Camelback Road in Phoenix, the 6:00 p.m. group of ten respondents entered the room. The client and I were behind a one-way window, confidently eating lasagna and drinking beer. The food is usually very good at focus groups; I've had many clients who carefully review the menu weeks in advance of the session!

After approximately 20 minutes of exposing those ten target consumers to a completely realistic product mock-up, I sensed the session was not going well. The participants were asking very basic questions about the product, the answers to which should have been clear. The next thing I recall was the client nudging me gently with his elbow inquiring, "What's wrong with these people? They don't get it."

"Bad group. It's just a bad group," I responded. I was beginning to sweat a bit but was careful not to let on that I was concerned. At a time like this, you try to think of reasons to blame it on the group moderator's methodology or to fault the group itself. When that doesn't work—as in this case—you simply hope like hell that the second group reverses the first. That does happen, but it's rare, and intuitively I knew it was not likely this time. This was straight-forward stuff: simply show the concept, listen to what they say, then probe them for the details behind their comments.

Twenty minutes into the second group I got the same nudge and comment from the client. At that point, my options were few: I could accept responsi-bility for creating a loser or blame the city of Phoenix and its citizens. For a brief moment I remember thinking that the hot desert air had probably nega-tively affected the group's thinking, making them even more cynical than usual. But I thought better of it, knowing that this excuse would never fly.

As you can see, I was not thinking clearly. Despite my well-cultivated ego, I knew I had to suck it up and accept the fact that I had failed. I use "I" here because, while the client had a significant level of buy-in to our creative, I was clearly on my own at this point.

Flying back to L. A., I had a breakthrough that altered my way of creating forever. I realized that the target consumer had been missing in our creative process. We had been developing concepts based upon research, client input, all of our collective experiences and all of our combined egos. We had con-sidered everything but the target consumer. If you understand why that's a flawed approach, then we're on the same page.

Up until then, I had always hated awaiting research results, and when they ar-rived, if they were negative, I would for the most part blame the messenger— the researcher. We were good, but now and then we had to suffer the remorse of performing poorly in research. That remorse has to be experienced to be appreciated; it's like giving birth to a baby nobody likes.

For instance, suppose you are the parent of a newborn baby. You have created this child and contemplated its arrival with an intense degree of emotional attachment. You walk down the hospital hallway with your spouse to look through the window into the room where all the newborns are kept. When you get there, it's crowded with other parents and relatives and all you can do is wait behind the crowd and observe until the others leave.

You soon notice that all of these people are making fun of your new creation. You are appalled, but they don't leave for two hours (the length of an average focus group)! To make it worse, your mother-in-law (the client) shows up, and for the two hours until the heckling stops, you feel compelled to address every criticism made. As you do, your mother-in-law simply rolls her eyes. Under the circumstances, there are only two possible responses from her: "I thought so" or (worse) "I told you so." In any case, your mother-in-law just became a distant relative.

Before I landed in Los Angeles, I made a career-altering decision. Noticing that the target consumer was not included in our creative process, I developed a new methodology to correct that. I will share this "team" approach later in the book so you can profit from it as well.

It's accurate to say that every idea in this book is a result of our ongoing experience with target consumers. It is just as true to say that every one of these ideas was born out of a fear of failure—an ever-present wish to never again be rejected by a focus group. This has profoundly improved the quality of our work. Subsequently, I no longer fear the results of research, which has greatly improved the quality of my life.

Incidentally, the product was eventually put on hold upon the realization that its availability would have seriously eroded the sales of one of the client's other top-selling products. For that reason, I doubt this product will ever make it to market.

Ownership is Fickle

Taking what we all thought was a strong concept to Phoenix and failing ultimately brought the understanding that we needed to incorporate the target consumer into our process. The experience also revealed to me the nature of ownership (i.e., ownership of any new concept). By ownership, I mean credit for the idea, not who owns the product.

From well before Phoenix to the day we presented the initial array of ideas to the client, the concepts were routinely referred to as the Chambers concepts.

That's us…The Chambers Group. At that point the client felt we had done a good job of identifying possible opportunities, though the "killer" positioning approach had not yet emerged. As we refined, merged, purged and experimented with the array of concepts, one began to coalesce. As it did, it began to build support and soon became the client's concept. Their confidence in the idea was high and they were willing to take responsibility for its existence. It did not, however, take long for its ownership to revert abruptly back to us that day in Phoenix.

The ownership of an idea is a funny thing—if the idea is "good" (i.e., clearly destined to be successful with consumers), it quickly becomes the property of many people as it passes through the final steps of the research that validates it. At the end of the process, it often becomes the brainchild of senior management. After a successful launch, it develops into the brainchild of everyone in the company. At that point I have become, for the most part, invisible—at least that's how it feels to me.

A case in point is Orville Redenbacher's "Movie Theatre Butter" popcorn a few years back. In the early phases of its development, it had virtually no parents. By the time it was introduced and was an apparent hit, it began to develop a significant family of marketers who claimed intimate involvement. About six months after its launch, it had grown the Redenbacher brand share by 10%! Upper-level executives, it seems, are as even-handed about taking credit as they are about handing out blame. In this case, an undeserved amount of credit was bestowed upon a marketing director who was promoted to company president for his perceived success.

Typically, one individual mentors a project and is ultimately responsible for its success or failure. As you may have guessed, it is not always the right person. There were, of course, many people involved in this particular triumph. A few months after the launch, when the success of the product was well documented, *Brandweek* magazine ran an article that gave credit to everyone but the lady who deserved it. That lady now resides in Temecula, California. I trust this will serve as recognition for your great work, Maryruth.

Why I'm Giving Away the Keys
Chapter Three

The Pitch

If you have ever made a business presentation, pitched an idea to a friend, faced the occupant of the car in front of you that you just rear-ended, created a resume, gone out on a job interview, encountered a person you were attracted to at a social gathering or participated in an Internet dating service, you stand to gain significantly from what follows. All of the above circumstances have one compelling challenge in common: YOU want THEM to engage in your selling proposition and buy whatever it is you are selling. This characteristic is as fundamental to any business as it is to life itself.

Just as fundamental is the notion that "mine is better than theirs." That is to say, my product or service is better than my competition. My long-standing assertion that my creative service is better and thus offers more than my competitors do, has driven the evolution of my enterprise since its inception. Growing and constantly reinventing my services is an on-going process. In fact, there is nothing more fun and rewarding for me than when clients accept and work with the insights and methodologies I have created. That's something I never get complacent about. I am also eager to share my insights with potential clients particularly to see their reactions to what they consider a fresh approach to the "old school" methodology they've been working with for years. Having lived this way for a long time has caused me to become rather protective of what I constantly refer to as "our secrets". I'm eager to share them with established clients, but absolutely adamant about keeping them away from my competition.

That is, I was adamant. Here's how all of that changed.

When you are selling something, the world seems to be made up of two kinds of people: prospects and customers. There are, of course, many other important groups of people on the planet, but if you are selling, these are the two that you must communicate with effectively in order to succeed.

Customers are those special people buying your product or service. However, before customers become customers they are prospects. In my world, customers and prospects are as different as night and day. I love my customers, but the best I can do for my prospects is tolerate them. My experience is that the truest form of human transformation occurs when a prospect becomes a customer—now that's a beautiful thing.

That transformation is driven by one, and only one factor. That factor is in your hands. It occurs when your prospect is exposed to your selling proposition and is so affected by it that they transform into a customer. Your selling proposition is delivered by your pitch and if it's effective, success will follow.

Recently, at the request of a long-standing client, I gave a capabilities presentation to him and two of his new partners. The capabilities presentation explains what we do, whom we do it for and the results that we routinely produce. It takes about 35 minutes. They had recently formed an enterprise that would develop and market new products in the ever-expanding and dynamic beverage category. They were well funded and ready to put the company on the fast track.

Steve, the client, had recommended our group based largely upon our branding and positioning skills and our past history of performing well for him. I could tell he was eager for our group to be accepted by his new partners.

I recognized one of his partners as someone who had risen to the top of two well-known consumer goods companies. I suspected that this new venture was likely funded largely upon his participation. The second partner was introduced as an advertising executive turned marketing consultant, a man named Archie with an impressive list of credits.

Over time, and after many such presentations, I have trained myself to read everyone in the room carefully, always giving primary attention to the one or two who I perceive are not enrolled in what I am pitching. "Enrolled" is a word not often used this way but one that communicates the essence of this particular situation and affords the opportunity to highlight its importance. "Enrolled" infers that the person you are speaking to has fully accepted what you are saying as true. Beyond that, they are inspired to support you in the achievement of your objective. That's the important part.

(Note that as you read on I will be distinguishing many words and concepts in order to facilitate your understanding of this material. In most instances, my definitions will not quite sync with those you may find in the dictionary. Many of my definitions have been customized to accommodate the world of marketing and to distinguish new insights that I have revealed.)

On this day, the two new guys both seemed enrolled, so I was feeling pretty good about myself. Their enrollment became obvious to me the moment they began discussing events well beyond that of deciding to work with us. I could tell that working with us was a given. My confidence allowed me to have fun with the presentation, and that in turn, normally means it is perceived as much more powerful than when I'm straining to get my message across. Having fun is the single most effective way to enroll others in whatever you are pitching. Simply put, people want to hang out with others who are having fun.

But enrolling others is not always so easy. My experience of presenting my credentials hundreds of times is that three, and only three, types of prospects are possible. Even in the face of a powerful, skillfully delivered presentation, these three keep showing up: the activist, the pacifist and the indifferent.

The Activist

The activist is the one I'm always after and prepared to embrace. These people seem to have "cracked the code" even before I present the material. They have a clear understanding of what we provide, know how it applies to them and are eager to get started. They have enrolled themselves. I have always considered them to be at least a touch enlightened; the clouds in their business lives have parted and they see us as a direct access to success. On top of that, they have the courage to move forward.

Put another way, they appear to have been looking for us.

As it turned out that day, Archie, the advertising guy, was one of the enlightened elite. He not only got it, but he got it to such an extent that he pulled me aside and requested we talk privately after the meeting. That request seemed unusual from someone I had only just met.

During our private conversation, I discovered that Archie not only saw our work as it applied to the project but understood that it had applications far beyond. I recall him saying, "Buddy, I don't know if you realize what you have here, but these are the keys to the vault." He wanted to know if I was interested in selling my company and, in the same breath, suggested that I seriously consider writing a book.

You see, Archie, who had to sign a non-disclosure agreement just to see the capabilities presentation, was impressed by my track record and immediately felt the technology that produced it, should be shared. I smiled and thanked him, and recall thinking to myself that my writing a book would guarantee my competition immediate access to all that I have worked so hard for throughout my professional life. What a bad idea! It seemed completely out of character to have come from someone I thought was so enlightened. Archie was a committed activist but he clearly was not thinking about my professional well-being, and I dismissed his idea completely. At that time I felt strongly that this was the reason our loyal clients kept coming back; I was protecting the trade secrets I had developed.

That was my initial reaction, anyway. More about Archie later.

The Pacifist

The second reaction to a portfolio presentation involves the pacifist. They are similar to activists in that they also have a clear understanding of what we provide, as well as a pretty good understanding of how it applies to them. Unfortunately, both of those insights are followed by a blinding and seemingly perpetual skepticism. Over time, I have discovered that this particular form of skepticism is driven by an overwhelming insecurity. Pacifists are committed to being doubtful yet are in complete denial about it. They are faced with what I call a painful dilemma.

Once exposed to the information, they now possess the knowledge that we consistently perform well for others and will likely do the same for them. However, they will be accountable if they take the action required to allocate funds and initiate the project. They see that the safest thing to do is to do nothing, yet are torn by the presence of an opportunity with a strong probability of success. The dilemma is that if they kill the project early on it might tip off the boss that they are not the aggressive marketer that their resume purports. On the other hand, they are also aware that the organization has been using a different methodology, one that has consistently produced poor results. If they revert back to that tactic they have a "no-fault" pass because poor results are accepted. Faced with a dilemma of this magnitude, a skilled pacifist does what they have trained themselves to do—they initiate "the stall".

Once they are in stall mode, they're safe. They're in action but not at risk. They are comfortable again. They are actually "lit up"—energized—by their relentless pursuit of reasons not to move forward. They will never let go of the idea that the project might still move ahead; if they did that, they would have no reason to impede the project. The skill with which they execute the stall is impressive. They tell themselves they merely have to get all their "ducks in a row" before moving forward. In this case, we must be talking about ten fast, aggressive ducks loose on a football field with just one pacifist trying to line them up. You can see it may take some time… perfect! If they can convince others that the ducks are loose, they can recommend more research to get them in order. Can't make a decision until then. Research in this context becomes the perfect dodge against making a decision. I have many research friends who are often frustrated with marketers who ask for more investigation when it is simply not indicated.

In Corporate America, the pacifist can always count on one thing for sure: the life-saving "reorganization". It's always just around the corner and will put an end to all the duck hunting. The pacifist moves on to a new job responsibility and the project goes into the file where it becomes an endeavor without a mentor. The stall is over until it is needed again.

The Indifferent

However well I thought I understood the first two types, I confess that I had zero understanding of the third group, the indifferent. These are the people who, in the face of a powerful, skillfully delivered presentation with overwhelming evidence to support it, seem not to have been in the room. Their indifference is almost creepy. They are uninterested at the start of the presentation and remain so throughout. To present to the indifferent is a character-building exercise. Even the presence of only one indifferent person in a group of ten is confounding to the most experienced presenter. A few months back, it was a group of seven indifferent marketers who kicked my butt for what I promised myself would be the last time…it wasn't.

Having said that, I will tip you off that these are the same folks I have to thank for the existence of this book. I feel a whole lot better about them lately, but I didn't back then.

It started when I got a call from an advertising executive in Chicago who wanted to refer us back to an account of his. Right off, that makes him an activist. With an activist on the brand team, we were the front-runners for sure. This client was a major consumer goods marketer located in New Jersey. I felt we were in a great position to get this particular project, as several years back this same advertising executive had referred us to the same account. That time we created a new brand for a significant segment of their business, which had since been declared an unqualified success by both the agency and client. That brand has now become a household word among target consumers in its category. So how could we possibly miss?

Well, this time it went down quite differently. For one thing, there were more people involved in the pitch phase. They put together a team consisting of seven people from five of their departments. The assignment was essentially to reorganize a large segment of approximately 100 existing products.

There were three areas to address. The first was to pull all 100 products together under one brand and position them as a superior alternative to their competition—"position", meaning we would develop a powerful message that would be communicated to the target consumer. It would be a message that would stimulate trial and encourage repeat purchase. The second was to individually distinguish each product in an otherwise fairly generic group of ordinary ones. Thirdly, we had to organize all the products into a common packaging structure. This arrangement would give rise to a significant display area that would communicate the new brand and its fresh positioning scenario.

It seemed a perfect fit for us. We knew from experience that the first two areas of the assignment involved growing sales and profits, which were clearly our domain. That's also the area that normally gets the attention of marketers; after all, who doesn't want increased sales and profits? The third area—packaging structure—is important, too, but in a secondary way; though not likely to generate significant new business, a great structure can make life easier by providing a strong billboard for whatever brand and product positioning we create.

The initial presentation was for the purpose of presenting our capabilities. A detailed proposal was to be developed and presented in the future, provided we made the "cut". And, we always make the cut—always.

In structuring our presentation, I made a conscious decision to thoroughly cover our ability to deliver in all three areas with a strong emphasis on the first two. As I said, I had decided that the first two areas were far more important than the third because they directly impacted sales and profits. I flew to New Jersey with a high degree of confidence that we would prevail. How could we not?

The day of the presentation came and I opened with the observation that the project objective was to increase sales and profits. Ninety-nine out of a hundred times that is a valid general observation that will garner cheers from the client. In this case, the client team nodded. Just nodded. And they were polite nods, too, as in "not-approving-at-all". I repeated the statement a second time and received the same reaction. Even the advertising guy, my activist buddy, had a blank look on his face. I remember thinking to myself, "Damn, I'm in some trouble here. Who are these people? Please God, not indifferents—not on this one!"

My confidence went out the window. It was bad enough that they did not react to the "increased sales and profits" objective, but they also rejected the three key points that followed which proved we were their direct access to success. At that point, I knew the remainder of the presentation held no hope of altering their initial response.

Now I know it's important for me to take full responsibility here, so I will. I blew it. I never blow it, but I did this time. A close friend of mine, a hard-core sales type, once told me that the key communication in a sales message is: "I have what you want." Whatever they were looking for, we clearly were not conveying to them that we had it or that we could even find it. Something went wrong that day and we did not make the cut. What was it? I thought about that for quite some time.

It took only three days to get word back that we had not made the cut. They say it's business and nothing personal, but if you're at all human, you take it on the chin. When you win it's personal and when you lose it's very personal. Oddly, though, I was mostly concerned that they might share what I had disclosed of our process to whomever else they choose to work with. You can see that by this time I had become a bit paranoid.

The Myth

It was shortly after that experience that I had lunch with my "activist" buddy Archie and got the breakthrough of my career. After I had drilled poor Archie about my experience with my pitch to the indifferents, he asked a couple of insightful questions. He asked why I had created these three groups of prospects. He went further and observed that I sounded like a critic reviewing Broadway plays. In that moment, I realized it was just the opposite. I was the Broadway play and I could not handle the critics. I loved them if they liked me but had to justify who they were if they rejected me. Archie's next question provided the breakthrough. He asked why I did not allow any of my staff to make portfolio presentations. My answer came in a second: "That's the fun part!" He responded: "Then, write the book." The drama was over. What could be more fun than writing the book? I now fully understood—this book would be the biggest pitch of my life.

Archie had been right after all. That's why I'm sharing all that I have discovered and why I'm excited at the possibility of having a large audience out there who will understand how it's done. I guess it took the New Jersey experience for me to rethink what I was doing; after all, I've noticed that shifts in our way of being only come about through our own experiences. This understanding has shifted my way of thinking forever about this technology, and I could not have come to this realization through a textbook. I had to have the experience to get the insight. I needed Archie's kick in the butt. Prospects are just people.

This is the Motivational Section

If you bought this book to get motivated that's okay but that is not at all what this book is about. This book is not intended to motivate you in any way and if it does, it is with no prior intention.

I attended a motivational conference when I was 28 and was truly "blown away" with the outcome. However, not "blown away" in the way you might imagine. I discovered that motivation is very short lived. It is impossible to hold on to. Meaning, you have to ask yourself if it has any value at all beyond feeling good for a short time.

My experience of motivation is that it is great fun. I personally consider motivation a form of recreation and I encourage you to classify it that way, too. This book is not about recreation. Motivation is external by nature and it feels good when it washes over you, but it is temporary at best. I can recall many times when I have been motivated. I enjoyed them all and I hope to experience more soon. My college team, Arizona State, won the Rose Bowl a number of years back and I remember feeling great for three days. I went on their website that day and bought $60 worth of stuff while under the influence of that particular motivation. I have not seen that stuff for some time now. Some music motivates me, and I have noticed that as long as it is streaming out of my *iPod* into my ears, it seems to last. I recently discovered that I can also get close to that feeling by firing down a couple cans of *Red Bull*, but that seems like cheating.

While I value motivation as a recreational experience, I do not know of any correlation between motivation and success. I do not anticipate success as a natural outcome of feeling motivated. I suspect someone could make a case for the value of being able to smile in the face of failure; personally, I recommend just being successful.

What I truly want for you to experience here is more internal and far more permanent by its very nature. As you read, you will obtain numerous insights, many of which will inspire you to make extraordinary changes in the way you conduct your business—transformations that will remain with you forever. It's the "discovery" that triggers the inspiration. When you realize something by yourself that you consider an extraordinary insight into your own life, you are, in a small way, changed forever. Over time, the excitement of the discovery will fade but the resulting shift in your thinking is where the ultimate value resides—and that lasts!

So, the goal is inspiration, not motivation. That's why I'm sharing these ideas with you. And that itself is something that inspires me.

The Marketing Objective
Chapter Four

Two Critical Functions

If you are going to convince consumers to purchase your product or service, you must successfully address two simple but critical marketing functions. You first must have an effective sales message and second, you must have your sales message exposed to a significant number of target consumers. It follows that if you have either one without the other, you will surely fail. In sophisticated marketing circles your sales message is referred to as your Selling Proposition and the point at which your target consumer is exposed to it is referred to as your Impact Point. All that you will do in your effort to successfully market your product or service, will occur within these two functions.

The Two Components of a Successful Selling Proposition

If I were to ask all the entrepreneurs I know to state their goal they would all say the same thing. In fact, I would get the same answer from my non-entrepreneurial friends as well. We are all looking for success. Yes, simply success. Over time, I have noticed two things that occur when success is present.

Together, these two things define all that is necessary for someone to be successful. This should not be confused with how to achieve success... that I have detailed in the remainder of this book. The two components of success apply to all businesses and are useful in setting the "Big Picture" context for what is to follow. So here it is—success is based upon your product or service:

1. Being initially perceived as unique; and

2. Immediately communicating a remarkable selling proposition.

That's it.

"Being initially perceived as unique" simply means that your product or service has the initial impact to get the attention of your target consumers. Without it, your selling proposition—your sales message—will never get the exposure it needs to perform its function. Without this initial perception of uniqueness, you will likely suffer.

"Immediately communicating a remarkable selling proposition" encompasses two fundamental assumptions that you need to be clear about. First, "immediately" means your selling proposition is easy for the target consumer to quickly comprehend. "Remarkable" means that your target consumer considers your selling proposition extraordinary compared to that of your competition.

Your Selling Proposition

Sophisticated marketers routinely use the term "selling proposition". They continuously construct it, scrutinize it, shape it, reshape it, re-scrutinize it and reconstruct it in an attempt to compete in a marketplace where their competitors are doing the exact same thing. It's a war among the giants. In your case, it is unlikely that your competition is even aware of their selling proposition—in fact; they probably don't even know the term. You are about to discover what an enormous advantage that is to you.

What a valid selling proposition means is that, at your price, your target consumer will purchase your product or service in adequate quantities to generate a reasonable profit for you. The selling proposition is comprised of all the words and graphics that you bring together to convince your target consumer to purchase your product or service.

The presumption—and it's a huge one—is that all of your target consumers are aware of your selling proposition and that you have communicated it powerfully. Such is seldom the case in the consumer goods and services industry.

It is rare to find it in the retail industry, as well, and it is simply missing in the Internet world. There is good news here. Due to the lack of basic understanding of the function of the selling proposition, your competition is vulnerable.

Creating that level of effective communication in the consumer goods and services industry is the main issue these businesses face daily. It is the very heart of all business. Without a powerful and effective selling proposition, any business will surely struggle and will likely fail.

If you are one of the millions of small business entrepreneurs in this country, then you are competing against others who don't have a clue about how to communicate a powerful selling proposition. Until now, that has been reserved for the big boys who can afford it. In other words, reserved for my clients. With this book, that is no longer the case.

If you have a truly great product or service and cannot, for the life of you, understand why consumers are not lined up around the block, you've come to the right place. I will demonstrate here what a powerful selling proposition can accomplish. The example I use is one I am quite familiar with given it is one of the classic battles that I have participated in. It concerns a consumer good that you, too, will surely know.

But first, there's something I'd like to say. Most likely your business is not selling a consumer good. Although consumer goods are heavily advertised and promoted, there are far more service and retail businesses. This book applies directly to these as well. I use consumer goods in a number of my examples because their selling propositions are on the faces of their packages, and are therefore easy to see, evaluate and understand. They are also good to study because the U.S. consumer goods market is the primary battlefield for all marketers worldwide; here in the States you find the best of the best.

As you continue reading, you will develop insights that will build your skills as an aggressive marketer, which will frequently be through the experience of what has transpired in categories other than yours. The learning will not be the same that you would experience in a textbook. Quite the opposite. It will be very experiential in nature and likely far more effective in developing your skills. It begins right here with me sharing the following experience.

The Power of the Selling Proposition

The sheer power and significance of the selling proposition has never been demonstrated more vividly than in the artificial sweetener category in the last few years.

Historically, this category has gone through many stages with consumers being jerked around by the federal government. More than once the feds banned key ingredients and later reversed their decision. Consumers were at the point where they believed that all of these products were potentially harmful, and were waiting for good news in the artificial sweetener category.

That good news came when *Splenda* was introduced by McNeil Nutritionals a few years back. At that time *Equal* was the category leader and most

consumers thought it was the best of the lot. *Splenda* featured three words in its selling proposition and everything changed overnight.

What were the magic words? "Made from sugar." Those words were all consumers needed to hear for them to jump ship immediately and abandon *Equal*. The *Splenda* selling proposition was communicated with those simple words and some graphics on the front of the package. *Splenda* did not need anything more to pull it off; we consumers were waiting for "made from sugar" to make using an artificial sweetener all right. What is truly human of us is that we did not consider what was behind those words; we were so eager for this product to be good for us that we didn't bother to look further. Can you see that this is all based on perception? Your selling proposition is essentially about perception.

So, let's look behind those words at the absurdity of this case study.

First off, do any of you actually believe that within a group of heavily processed products such as artificial sweeteners, that there's one, which is truly better for you than any of the others? Do you think that, except for their lack of calories, any one of them could be considered good for you? Hello! Pour them out and compare them. Does *Splenda* look any more like sugar than the others? Of course not. Yes, technically *Splenda* is made from sugar, but it is also processed with a chlorine derivative. I recently googled *Splenda* and the first article I noticed was entitled, "The Lethal Science of *Splenda*, a Poisonous Chlorocarbon" by James Bowen, M.D. Admittedly, I did not bother to read the article nor can I vouch for its accuracy, but you get the point. This is what a powerful selling proposition can do.

That's right—chlorine. As anyone knows who has ever been in a hot tub or a swimming pool, chlorine is one of the most caustic chemicals known to man. The success of *Splenda* is one for the marketing case study courses of the future as a sterling example of the power of the selling proposition. My advice to you is that the next time you are choosing an artificial sweetener, do it solely on the basis of taste and not on its prior relationship to sugar. With enough chemistry applied to it, I suspect sugar can be turned into anything.

Can you see how much more important your selling proposition is than even your product or service? Having a great product, relative to success, guarantees nothing. Can you see that success can hang on just two or three words? I suspect that "Made from sugar" will be of little value to you in marketing your product or service; in fact, it is very difficult to discover exactly what words or graphics will "trigger" your target consumer. That challenge is exactly what this book is about—to help you create and validate those kinds of powerful "triggers" for your business.

I'm fairly sure that your marketing situation is not quite as competitive as in the artificial sweetener category. If three words can make such a significant difference in that outrageously competitive environment, I assure you that you can find the triggers for your business that will produce extraordinary results as well.

Remember, the good news is that no matter what your product or service, most marketers (ideally your competition) are generally unaware of the potential of the selling proposition. I'd estimate that less than 3% of all products and services are powerfully communicated to their targets.

There is no reason for you not to be in that rare and unique 3%. Believe me, life is good in the 3% zone!

Your Impact Point

Your "impact point" is the place where your selling proposition is most frequently exposed to your target consumer. It is where your target will evaluate your selling proposition and make a decision to purchase or pass. The best examples to illustrate this are 1) consumer goods, 2) retail businesses and 3) Internet businesses. All three have their impact point at the same location as their "point of sale". That's incredibly convenient and a huge advantage over all other businesses where the impact point is not at the point of sale. For those businesses, the impact point is typically some form of advertising or promotion such as a billboard for an insurance company or law firm.

All products and services have multiple impact points. For instance, if you were operating a dry cleaning company, your sales message is conveyed when target consumers encounter your store front, your *Yellow Pages* ad, your brochure and your website. Your key impact point is the one that you consider most important. Typically, that is the impact point that has the greatest exposure. Let's assume for the dry cleaning business it is the storefront.

It's easy to see that the target consumer for *Splenda* is impacted by the product package sitting on a supermarket shelf. The target consumer makes a decision and acts on it immediately. For a movie, its impact point is the poster, the newspaper ad and/or trailer, in which case the buying and purchasing decisions are separated in time and space. For a retail business, the key impact point is probably the storefront; for an Internet business, it's homepage or a banner ad. For *Roto-Rooter*, it's their ad in the *Yellow Pages* or on TV. For a radio station or TV show, it might be a billboard, and for a janitorial service, a brochure. For a rock star, it's the cover of a CD. If you were publishing a book, it would be the cover, of course, and your sales would depend largely on how well you executed your selling proposition.

Let's look closer at the word "impact" in the term "impact point". There were two components of success that you reviewed earlier of which the first was "being initially perceived as unique". That perception is critical in calling attention to your selling proposition. Your message must be designed in such a way as to have your product or service initially perceived as a clear alternative when compared to your competition's. If accomplished, it will trigger the awareness and, in turn, the curiosity necessary in your target consumer so that they will engage in your selling proposition.

You have no doubt heard the term "think outside the box". One of the best examples I know relative to creating an impression at the impact point came to me a few months back when I developed the need to put new soles on a pair of old boots that I did not want to give up. I hadn't visited a shoe repair shop in at least four or five years, yet it took but a split second to think of one about a half mile from my office. I had no recollection of its name or services, but I had no trouble visualizing exactly where it was.

If you look closely at the photo to the right, which was taken before 9:00 a.m., you can see that the shop looks like any other store; poorly defined to be sure. In fact, the cleaners next door is clearly getting most of the attention on this block.

Now, check out the second photo and notice the shift that takes place around 9:01 a.m., when it becomes legal to park on the street. The cleaners's sign still works, but for the remainder of the day, anyone who passes becomes much more aware of where to go the next time

they need some work done on their shoes. This is what I call "out of the box" impact at its best. This guy sets the bar pretty high; now you and I have to live up to it.

Multiple Impact Points

Multiple impact points further complicate the task of communicating your selling proposition. Many have widely varied impact points depending on the category they're in. Humans, as it turns out, have only one impact point. That is, humans who are not celebrities, but people like you and me. That point is the experience that others have in the course of a normal one-on-one encounter. If you take time to check it out, you will quickly discover that humans position themselves in exactly the same way we have trained ourselves to position our products and services.

Given that multiple impact points are the norm, it is important to distinguish which impact point is most important to your business. That is usually a simple matter of determining which impact point gets the most number of exposures to your target consumer.

Having made that choice, I recommend you concentrate your thinking on that particular impact point as you continue reading. I further recommend you declare that impact point the official communication of your sales message and any consideration that you have for your sales message in the future, have it always be as it applies to that impact point. This focus will serve you well over time. You will of course make adjustments to all of your remaining impact points as appropriate for each.

We have been associated with the marketing of an animated DVD that is targeted to toddlers. We centered the marketing and sales of it around a website but determined that the home page was secondary in importance when compared to the email flyer ad. The ad that follows was designed to sell the product without consideration to the homepage. Clicking on the "Order Now" button will take target consumers immediately to the order form. For the target consumers who need detailed information beyond the ad, they will simply click on the homepage address at the bottom of the page. Our intention is that they order first and only do that as a last resort.

When considering impact points and communicating selling propositions through them, one new product experience really stands out for me. In 1989, I was given an assignment that, to this day, I consider an extremely difficult communications challenge given its two impact points. In fact, it remains the most difficult selling scenario of my career. There was no established category for this product, given that it performed a function never before envisioned by tar-

get consumers. Additionally (and not to confuse you), its multiple impact points needed to be communicated on its primary impact point—its retail package.

The product was a retail electronic item. As it turned out, our generic descriptor created the name for the category, for which there would never be a second entry. Most marketers would agree that, under nearly all circumstances, you are far better off having competition than having your product or service forced to support the category alone. In fact, if there is no second entry, all you have is a lone product or service and, technically, you don't even have a category. The generally accepted definition of a category is that it is made up of a group of products or services that compete with each other by performing a similar function. This product was new technology based upon the consumer complaint that programming a VCR was difficult, if not impossible, for many.

When I first met the product's inventor, Henry Yuen, there were four employees in his company, including himself. Henry had named his company

Gemstar long before I arrived on the scene. Of all the people I have encountered in my career, Henry had far and away the most impressive educational credentials. He earned a B.S. in Mathematics at the University of Wisconsin, a Ph.D. in applied mathematics at the California Institute of Technology (CalTech) and, to top it off, a law degree from Loyola University School of Law. Add to this an intuitively aware and inquisitive mind and nerves of steel and you have Henry Yuen. His partner Daniel Kwon was based in Hong Kong where he was well established as a manufacturer of electronic hardware. Henry hired us to develop the strongest possible selling proposition for his new product.

This new product enabled TV viewers to pre-select programs based upon entering code numbers into a battery-operated device that sat atop their VCRs. The code numbers were found in the TV listing section of all major newspapers, and pivotal to the product's success was getting *TV Guide* to print them as well.

The assignment was to communicate all aspects of this complicated selling proposition on its key impact point—its retail package. We knew that there would be little advertising support making the impact point communication task critical to the product's success. Not only did we need to identify a new category and what the product did, we also needed to include the newspaper code listings into the selling proposition. Those listings were a second impact point located in the publications, but were of little value in communicating the product. The publications were adamant about the space they were already giving up for the numbers and would not allow any additional sales message. The target consumer would only find numbers in the listings with no explanation of why they were there.

First came the name. We settled on *VCR Plus*, which, in retrospect, could have been construed as somewhat misleading if the consumer got too literal; it sounds like a VCR with some additional function added to it. In spite of this, it turned out to be a great brand name. The generic descriptor, "Instant Programmer", also functioned as the key performance attribute assuming one had read the name "*VCR Plus*" first. "Instant Programmer" also establishes the category, while the benefit "Makes Taping Easy" says it all, with the rest of the copy all about how you use it. The answer to the "how" question was organized into a window that explained what to do and also displayed the familiar *TV Guide* listing layout of that era.

The success of this product lay with Henry's cunning and ingenuity. Getting publications to print the code numbers and pay Gemstar a fee for doing so was brilliant. Accomplishing that feat came right down to the wire; we were well into the launch phase when we got the last of three critical cities: New York, Chicago and Los Angeles. It could have easily failed right there. *TV Guide*, if I recall correctly, was the last to sign up based solely on the fact that they realized they were about to be left out. For the most part the newspapers were also afraid of being

left out once they realized that Henry was serious about launching his product. If the product took off, they would have looked stupid in the public eye given that their entire selling proposition is based on publishing TV listings with complete information. And so, reluctantly, they all published the code numbers.

The initial hardware release was only the first phase of the business plan. Once *VCR Plus* was introduced and considered a success, it was followed by the licensing of the technology for installation by other manufacturers as original equipment. This was accomplished fairly smoothly and was critical, since the initial retail unit hardware had many performance problems. By the third year, the retail unit had become less important to the grand scheme of *VCR Plus* as many VCRs, including those made by *Sony* and *Panasonic*, entered the market with *VCR Plus* technology included.

The "installed base" was always an important number to Gemstar, and a closely guarded secret. The "installed base" was the term coined to identify the volume of hardware in the hands of consumers. It is a major factor in the electronic game category, with the *Microsoft Xbox* being a great example. Its installed base is so significant that many independent manufacturers like Electronic Arts, Activision and others are more than willing to create software for it. (You may have noticed that *Sega*, in recent years, has abandoned its production of hardware in favor of producing software for other hardware systems.)

As it turned out, *VCR Plus* was only the beginning for Henry. I was never more surprised than in 1991 when he disclosed what we later called I Plus. It was an ingenious idea that should and would have worked if the installed base had been more clearly identified and addressed.

I Plus was a new advertising media alternative for advertising agencies to reckon with. Imagine you see an ad for the new Chevrolet Corvette in the newspaper, and at the bottom, there's a bold note telling you that if you want more information, including where the local dealers are, you simply enter the following *VCR Plus* code into your VCR. Your VCR then picks up a short infomercial in the middle of the night, a time when few people are watching TV, but, more importantly, when TV time slots are cheap to buy. Think about it; it is advertising targeted at people already interested in a product—what smart entrepreneur wouldn't want to take advantage? The concept was launched, but did not fly, primarily because there was no way to validate the number of exposures. That made it impossible for advertising agencies to appraise its value. I believe, with the right technology, it could still be a valid advertising methodology. It was clearly ahead of its time, and its time may have finally arrived. Recently *TiVo* and *Yahoo!* announced a joint venture to launch a service similar to that of I Plus. In addition, *DIRECTV* is offering a pop-up icon on some commercials that gives viewers—just like I Plus—the option to get additional information by pressing the "Thumbs Up" button on their *TiVo*. Henry was exactly 20 years ahead of his time—but that's Henry.

There is an epilogue to the Henry and Gemstar story. As time went on, TV Guide continued to give him a hard time about printing and paying for the codes. A year or so after Gemstar was listed on the NYSE, Henry successfully purchased *TV Guide*, ending that squabble forever.

Being Aggressive

Most of us in the business world would agree that being aggressive is a virtue. In fact, we might concur that it's essential for success. Most people, particularly my clients, characterize me as aggressive, and given my earlier description of myself as a "hired gun", you can probably conclude that I don't disagree with them. The origin of my aggressiveness is my constant and continuing association with aggressive—and, might I add, successful—marketers. During the time that Henry and I worked together, I observed his ability to identify multiple opportunities and pursue all of them with the energy and efficiency that most people might only muster for one. I immediately recognized the value of such a comprehensive approach to one's business—it ensures a far greater chance of overall success. It also keeps you from getting attached to any one project, making the mistake of over-managing it, getting too personally attached or falling into any number of other traps. You need to know when to drop a business venture and move on.

But, let me qualify the above: aggressiveness is a virtue only if intelligently directed. Ultimately, Henry's aggressiveness turned into aggression, which is not the same. Henry's hostility apparently went beyond what I encountered while working with him in his *VCR Plus* days, since it landed him in quite a bit of trouble. While *VCR Plus* was a great example of aggressively creating the impact necessary for success, Henry went a bit too far.

By the late 1990s, Henry had taken Gemstar public and built it into a company with a net worth of more than $3 billion. In October 2002, Henry and his company fell under the scrutiny of the Securities and Exchange Commission (SEC). Gemstar was accused of accounting fraud to the tune of $248 million. As a result of the investigation, Henry was fired from Gemstar in April 2003 and, soon after, was indicted by the Justice Department. According to Randall Lee, the SEC's Pacific Regional Director, Henry "intentionally and willfully destroyed key evidence relevant to a core issue in the investigation: his knowledge of and participation in the fraud at the company."

A plea bargain was worked out with the Justice Department for Henry to pay a $250,000 fine, donate $1 million to charity, receive three years probation and serve six months of home detention—a proposal heavily criticized by the SEC and thereby rejected by the court. After a three-week trial in December 2005, the court found in favor of the commission, and ordered Henry to pay $22 million in disgorgement and penalties. The decision was upheld again in April 2008.

It is difficult for me to imagine how Henry, given his intelligence and experience, could end up in so much trouble. Of course, I'm sorry to say that at this time in our history, he's not the only one who has broken the law because of greed. With this in mind, I say be aggressive in every aspect of running your business, but beware of aggression. Both *Webster* and I define "aggressive" as "taking committed action" and "aggression" as "taking hostile action." There is a definite difference.

The Creative Side—
Positioning and Repositioning
Chapter Five

I have been in creative marketing for more than 30 years, and in that time have assembled an extraordinary team. We consider ourselves proficient in three areas: new product and service development; new product and service positioning; and established product and service repositioning.

Many people think that creating a new product or service idea and launching it is the most effective way to generate new business. That has not at all been my experience. If you have an existing business, the least expensive and most effective way to create incremental revenue is to reposition the product or service you are currently selling. Simply put, you are going to sell more of what you already have. You have already created the business and covered your overhead, so each additional dollar of business represents new profit. Although I do refer to the product development function on occasion, I have devoted this book to the positioning function of launching a new business and the repositioning function of growing an existing business.

New Product and Service Development

In this area, we develop new product or service concepts. On a typical project, we will present from eight to twelve concepts that will be subjected to qualitative research, usually focus groups. After narrowing the concepts down and refining those favored by the client, the stronger ones are submitted to volumetric research. That is where large numbers of target consumers are exposed to the concept. At this point the notion exists, but the physical product has yet to be developed. Developing the product comes after consumer tests indicate a strong affinity for the idea. Those results are taken into consideration and further refinements are made. At that point, the decision is made whether or not to develop the physical product based upon volume projections. Once the physical product or service is developed, additional "hands on" product tests will determine if it gets launched. These tests are typically conducted by allowing the target consumer to use and react to the actual product or service. Although this is a significant part of my business, new product and service development is not the subject of this book. The second and third areas, positioning and repositioning, represent far greater opportunities for success, so I will focus on them. I will, however, take time here to share with you a product development scenario I run into often, as it may be of value. It involves individuals with new product ideas who ask me to evaluate them and possibly refer them to the appropriate company.

The Inflated Value of Ideas

In the creative world, an idea is worth absolutely nothing. On the other hand, the execution of the idea is of extraordinary value. So you could say up to this point, the insights you have gained here are worth absolutely nothing. What I have shared with you so far are a series of distinctions and abstractions that may have led you to certain insights. These observations, while they are critical to your success, are just like ideas—absolutely worthless. Only their execution is of value. On the other hand, given the quality of those insights, their implementation may be of extraordinary value if you know how to carry it out.

To prove my point, let's take a literal look at a "worthless" abstraction. It is never more evident than in the motion picture industry. I am going to pitch a new idea for a film and you judge the value of it.

A couple in their late thirties reside in a small New England town where he's an aspiring college professor and she's a stay-at-home mom raising their two boys, 8 and 12. He has an affair with a student. She catches him and leaves, taking the kids with her to her mom's. They soon make up and she and the kids return home. Soon thereafter she is diagnosed with cancer and dies.

Good idea or bad? Sounds unremarkable to me, and most producers would probably agree.

This idea for a film was executed in 1983. It was executed well enough to garner eleven Academy Award nominations, and won five Academy Awards. Can you see that all of the value is in the execution? The film, of course, was *Terms of Endearment.*

Do not get discouraged. What this means is that when you get that great idea, be realistic. Given it is worthless as is, you simply need to add value to it. That can be done in a number of ways. You can develop it, and the further you do, the more value it will take on. If it can be patented, that is huge, but not at all necessary. Notice that very few products and services are protected with patents. If your idea is a new cookie, it is fruitless to go for a patent, as it will be rejected. You can, however, package it and sell it in a small local restaurant. If it succeeds, you can move it to a regional grocery chain. At that point you may get a call from Sara Lee and retire. I guarantee you that Sara Lee would not have been interested in your original idea.

Here's one more example. You are probably aware of the story of MySpace. Do you think Rupert Murdoch would have been interested in that idea? No way. However, he eventually paid $580 million.

Throughout the remainder of this book, I will often use the term "product or service". When I do, I mean for you to interpret it in the broadest possible sense. What is important is that the technology I am sharing with you will apply directly to you and your business regardless of what you are selling. Throughout my career I have personally worked with products and services within a large number of categories. I have listed some of those products and services for your review. If I am an expert, it is not in any single category but rather in the process that may bring success in any category…yours!

- National beauty pageant (Miss America)

- Cat litter (*Arm & Hammer*)

- Feature animation
  (*Cheech & Chong's Smokin' Animated Movie*)

- Line of snack bars (*General Mills*)

- Artificial sweetener (*Equal*)

- Line of bottled waters (*Sparkletts*)

- TV shows (Ultimate Gamer)

- Line of sandpaper (*3M SandBlaster*)

- Health and wellness resort (Genesis)

- Self-improvement educational seminars (Landmark Education)

- Breakfast cereals (*Chocolate Lucky Charms*)

- Physical fitness franchise (Weider Gyms)

- Animated DVD series (*SeaTales*)

- Line of condoms for men (*Trojan*) and women (*Trojan Her Pleasure*)

…and a whole lot more!

As I stated earlier, I will frequently use consumer goods as examples only because they are highly visible and, therefore, the easiest to understand for demonstration purposes. Whatever point I am making at the time will absolutely apply to your product or service as well. It will also fit for you whether you're a corporate executive or a street vendor, are in a retail business or selling a good or a service. When you see the words "product or service", trust me, I am referencing anything and everything that, in some way, needs to be sold.

Product and Service Positioning

The second area, positioning new products and services, consists of determining who the target consumer is and coming up with the words that define the basic nature of the message you want to convey to that consumer. This is typically contained in a document sophisticated marketers refer to as the "positioning statement". Over the years, I estimate that I have personally written four or five hundred such statements for my clients.

The positioning statement is located in the marketing file and is the inspiration used to generate all of the marketing communication tools by which your "selling proposition" is conveyed to your target consumer. The selling proposition is the message you are communicating at your impact point. It is the total communication that your target gets while driving past your building (if you are in the retail business), or the impression your target gets while walking down the supermarket or drugstore aisle (if you are selling a consumer product), surfing your homepage (if you are running an internet business) and so on.

My relationship to positioning statements has been strained at best, as intuitively, I have developed these overrated documents in a backwards manner when compared to accepted marketing methodology. Tradition has it that you work on your positioning statement until it is perfect, then hire a graphic designer or advertising agency to interpret it. On the surface, that may make perfect sense. Given that my early career was centered around package design, my training is based on the importance of creating the most powerful selling proposition as may be applied to the front of a consumer goods package. As I focused on the package design business, what evolved was a process that guaranteed creation of the most powerful selling proposition with little attention to the positioning statement. My method is based upon understanding the function of all the elements contained in a selling proposition and how to get target consumers to react to them positively at your impact point. Once that has been created, I use that to write the positioning statement.

These days when I enter a contract to develop a total marketing communication, both the positioning statement and selling proposition are included in the deliverables. What is unknown to many of my clients is that the very last thing I develop is the positioning statement, and that I create it by studying all the information I gather from target consumers while developing the selling proposition at the impact point. A positioning statement developed this way is far more accurate and thus far more powerful because it's based on the reality of the target consumers' input.

A researcher I work with told me that the idea of "playing with a positioning statement and automatically thinking you can replicate it at your impact point is now outdated." I absolutely agree. In other words, making adjustments to a document that characterizes your product or service is simply an academic exercise and does not mean you can replicate its message on a storefront or on the face of a consumer package. The only thing that matters is what is exposed to the target consumer at the impact point. Polishing a positioning document is only worthwhile as long as you understand it is not meant to show up as such on your product or service. Furthermore, there is a strong desire among marketers to understand the consumer thinking behind which communication elements they respond to. This, too, is relatively unimportant; what is critical is only that they respond in the first place. If all this seems academic to you, perfect…you are in the right place. For many of the world's most sophisticated marketers, however, the above might seem quite revolutionary.

Here is a simple analogy designed to demonstrate the function and importance of your selling proposition. Bananas currently sell for 45 cents a pound. So if you decide to get into the banana business, your selling proposition would be valid only if you could sell them at that price and make a profit. Your problem is how do you get target consumers to buy your bananas when *Dole* and *Chiquita* are your competition? The assumption is that your product or service will sell in adequate quantities to generate a profit if your selling proposition reaches the appropriate number of target consumers. It's up to you to confirm that. Once you do, it's up to me to show you exactly how to compete against *Dole* and *Chiquita* with a "remarkable positioning" scenario.

I will do exactly that.

The power of positioning is truly extraordinary. Positioning is the art of waging war using the arsenal of data that each marketer has at his or her disposal. The armory is comprised of all the facts about the category—specifically key competition for your product or service. The art is in understanding how to shape and mold that information into weapons you can use effectively.

I will define positioning more literally for you here and provide a second example of its sheer power. Positioning is "the words and graphics that combine to communicate your product's or service's selling proposition". You could say that the selling proposition is the product's message as interpreted by the target consumer.

I will share with you a positioning project that has been hard at work in the marketplace for many years. This positioning assignment came in 1982 from a company called *Knowledge Adventure*. The company was named after its first product, developed by company founder Bill Gross. Bill had developed what was one of the first children's educational software programs, and it was a hit. He had developed it specifically for his own kids.

Our assignment was to help position *Knowledge Adventure's* first curriculum-based product. It was targeted to kindergartners in a category whose leader at the time was *Reader Rabbit*. The *Reader Rabbit* line was extensive and covered grade levels from kindergarten through junior high school. Its position was based upon communicating the idea that children will be motivated by the "fun" nature of the rabbit character to actively participate and therefore learn.

The marketing team we were working with was very clear in its direction. They insisted we find a positioning scenario that, using a more personal appeal, would characterize the product as more effective than *Reader Rabbit*. What we created was *JumpStart Kindergarten* and it was a smash hit. It appealed, we believe, to the pressure that parents feel to see their kids get ahead of their peers. *JumpStart* software was seen as a way to obtain this result for their children.

That initial product, firmly positioned as described above, broke all existing sales records and became the inspiration for all of the *JumpStart* products that followed. The next time you are looking at educational software you may want to observe *JumpStart's* dominance, as well as the relative scarcity of *Reader Rabbit*.

100% Positioning

Now let's take a look back at the *Orville Redenbacher's* "Movie Theatre Butter" popcorn project, which you will soon see is 100% positioning as well. Having worked on the project, I am not at all sure there was any noticeable difference in the flavor profile of the "Movie Theatre Butter" product over the three butter-flavored products already on the shelf. It was simply more flavoring and a remarkable "Movie Theatre Butter" characterization. Can you see that "Movie Theatre Butter" popcorn at the movies is unremarkable, but, on that day in the microwave popcorn section of the supermarket, the target consumer saw it as absolutely remarkable? Can you determine a difference between Triple X Butter, Power Butter, Super Butter or any other butter relative to "Movie Theatre Butter"? I was there and "Movie Theatre Butter" was the only descriptor considered remarkable by the target consumer.

Based solely on that one product, *Orville Redenbacher's* market share grew from 30 to 40 percent in approximately six months. That's huge and it was all based upon the target consumer's perception. It was their reaction to the remarkable selling proposition of this new product and not to the configuration of the product itself.

When considering product or service versus selling proposition as possible areas of opportunity, rarely does a product or service breakthrough show up visually to the target consumer at the impact point. But when it does, well…it doesn't get much better than granola on top of a yogurt package.

As unique as the idea of putting granola on top of yogurt is, it was not a feature that could be protected. In fact, few products are protected by patents. There is far more proprietary opportunity in your selling proposition, and that is where the information in this book becomes a "deadly" weapon. Your weapon. While it is difficult to protect your product or service, you can own its name and often you can own how it is characterized by your selling proposition. Given a choice between a remarkable selling proposition and a remarkable product or service, I would take the remarkable selling proposition into battle every time.

The selling proposition is typically thought of as the executed form of the positioning statement. That's the positioning statement stashed away in the marketing filing cabinet. As discussed earlier, it is a statement carefully created by the marketing team and—theoretically—all of the marketing tools (for instance, advertising, P.R., promotion, etc.) used to sell the product or service should align themselves with that statement. For me, there is only one real selling proposition and it is the one in existence, meaning the one that is real and active in the mind of the target consumer and currently driving the product or service. That is the only selling proposition that counts—the one the target consumer says it is, end of story.

I have a female friend in her late thirties who is one of the most stunning ladies I have ever known. People often stare at her. As a result of all that attention, she has become truly shy. If you ask all of the people who routinely encounter her but don't know her, however, they will say she is a snob. She hates that and vehemently disagrees. This is a huge source of frustration for her as she is forced to deal with it constantly. So, is she a snob? Yes; shy is simply an illusion in her own mind. That's because the only impression that matters is the one in the minds of those she encounters. "Snob" is how she appears to other people and she's stuck with that until she takes action to reposition herself. If she were to write down the "shy" selling proposition scenario that she thinks applies to her, it would be no different from all of those well-groomed positioning statements in corporate marketing filing cabinets across America; they are, in fact, just selling proposition wannabes.

If you are making decisions based upon the positioning statement you have in your files without considering the true selling proposition, i.e., the one at work in the real world, you are operating at a big disadvantage.

Products and services by their very nature must be communicated through the selling proposition in order to be effective. In fact, your success is dependent upon how powerful your selling proposition appears to your target consumer. Your selling proposition, however, is not dependent upon your product or service at all. All that's necessary is that you have a product or service that ultimately fulfills the promise of your selling proposition. You can do just fine with an unremarkable product or service as long as you have a remarkable selling proposition. If you are struggling in your business, it is likely due to your target consumer's unremarkable perception of your current selling proposition.

Have you ever had the experience of buying a new product that you loved, only to discover when you went back a second time that it was not where you found it? That was most likely a remarkable product with an unremarkable selling proposition. If you think you were upset, imagine how its creator felt when it was pulled off the shelf due to poor performance. Without a remarkable selling proposition, a remarkable product will go unnoticed. The marketing graveyard is full of them.

It is impossible for target consumers to understand your product or service until they have been exposed to its selling proposition. If your product is inside of a jar, a can, a bottle, a brochure, a storefront or a box, this relationship is particularly true. If you are selling a service, it is also impossible to see it as it can only be experienced well after encountering its selling proposition. You can see how irrelevant any product or service becomes without a remarkable selling proposition.

As far as the target consumer is concerned, the product or service is an element of the selling proposition. For the most part, their initial exposure is the selling proposition. If they are not persuaded to engage at that point, they will never encounter the product. Granola on top of yogurt is one of those few occasions where target consumers could see the product before encountering its selling proposition.

Product and Service Repositioning

Area three—repositioning—is virtually the same as positioning except its purpose is to strengthen the existing position of a product or service currently in the market.

Even though we are skilled at developing new products, experience indicates the most significant new business opportunities are not rooted in new products at all. Launching new products is extremely costly and risky. Our experience is that, by comparison, there are far more opportunities and fewer risks in the world of repositioning existing products and services.

In all the years we have been in business, I do not remember two assignments completely alike. In addition, we always seem to be working on one or two projects that are fascinating in their own unique way. I will share with you a repositioning assignment that we recently initiated, though I will have to withhold the name of the brand since it remains a work in progress.

Repositioning assignments are often extremely challenging. They are normally based on changing the current selling proposition on an existing business with the objective of increasing consumer demand. This particular assignment does not conform to that scenario at all, which is why I am sharing it with you here.

This repositioning need is the result of an acquisition. Our client purchased a group of products that currently enjoy more than $100 million in annual gross sales. You would instantly recognize the brand as the undisputed leader within quite a large category, as these products are found in every drug store and supermarket in the country. One of the conditions of the sale, however, was that our client would only be allowed to use its current brand name for a period of three years. To make matters worse, the buying cycle is six to eight months. The buying cycle is the average time between purchases. That means the current target consumer has only limited exposure to the category. (Compare that to repositioning a brand of milk where the consumer visits the category on a weekly basis.) If we had a transition period where we had both the old and new brands on the package for six months, the milk consumer would have plenty of exposures to get used to the new name while our consumer on this brand would only see the interim package once. Surely you can see the dilemma. A new brand must be created to successfully replace the current one, one that has proven to be the most powerful ever in this category.

The consumer has fully acclimated to these products under their well-established brand name. This will be a delicate transition that must be executed perfectly or the target consumer will reject the new brand. "Cool" assignments like this are why I love this business. As I said, this is a work in progress so I can't report yet on the outcome, but it's definitely a good example of the many nuances of the repositioning function.

A Few Critical Insights
Chapter Six

There are a series of insights that generally apply to the world of marketing that typically take years to assimilate. Having them as a background will allow you to be significantly more effective at creating and managing your own success.

What's Next?

The secret to success with your product or service in your category is as much attitude as methodology. It is a working state of mind, an awareness that will give you a significant edge over your competition. You must adopt this state of mind since it's what makes the methodology powerful. Most of the marketers I come into contact with think that increasing their business is difficult, when in fact, it isn't at all. At least, not if you become responsible for "What's next?" Take note—this is where that working state-of-mind comes in.

First, let's get it straight with what I mean by "What's next?" "What's next?" is going to happen no matter what you do. Without having cracked open a book on the matter, I believe this to be a universal law of physics. It's just as certain as inertia; something different is coming. It will never again be as it is today. Categories evolve and nothing will prevent that. Most people think "What's next?" means new product innovation, and it certainly can. But far more often, the opportunity to grow your business is in the area of positioning or branding innovation. For that reason, we will deal in depth with both of these opportunities.

One simple way to look at positioning and branding is that they represent what you say about your product or service beyond its simple generic identification. Positioning typically refers to a single product, whereas branding pertains to a line of products.

An example of a brand would be *Yoplait* while the single product would be *Go-Gurt*. I can say with confidence that how you characterize your product or service is far more important than its reality. Can you see that it is much easier to change how you characterize your product or service than it is to change the product or service itself? It's also far less expensive.

The reality that many more opportunities exist in the realm of positioning and branding than in product or service development will be demonstrated clearly a bit later. I would say that for every new product or service opportunity, there are at least 40 positioning chances.

You see, what you want to get right here, right out of the box, is that it's about control. Controlling the category. Taking responsibility for "What's next?" is the key to ruling any category.

Now, I know how that sounds. But it is not necessary to be the number one brand, product or service in your category to control it. You do not have to be the "big guy"; in fact, you can make the big guy's life miserable. Your relationship to "What's next?" in your category is simple: You create it and drive the category or wait until someone else—probably the big guy—creates it, which means you suffer the effects of him having done so.

Consider for the moment the case of *Orville Redenbacher's* "Movie Theatre Butter" popcorn—a huge success based on three words. Having been a major part of that, I can tell you it would not have mattered which brand, large or small, came up with those three words; the success would have followed. There is nothing significant about the product other than more butter flavoring. All that matters is who comes up with the words.

We frequently run into categories where the client is convinced that everything has already been done. The category is presumed stagnant. The senior executives will be so certain of this that they will pull all marketing funds away from those brands. They will support what they perceive are products situated within growth categories. What they are missing is that the growth categories were also dormant until one of its brands created "What's next?" and brought it to life.

What most managers fail to see is that a dormant category represents a major opportunity. It's like having a blank canvas to create on. And it's easy to succeed given that senior managers of the competitive brands in these "dormant" categories are most likely to also pull marketing funds from their products. In a dynamic category, it is more difficult to anticipate competitive moves. In a static category, you can safely control a new way of characterizing your product or service with the confidence that your leveraging base (the category norms) are not going to change and that your competition will most likely not react to what you do in a timely fashion. Why? Because they, too, did not allocate resources to their brand in that category. If they have no funds to initiate "What's next?" it is doubtful they will have the money to react to what you do, either. The result is that blank canvas and you being the only dude with a brush. When you innovate within one of these dormant categories, you create "What's next?" So if your category is quiet, I suggest you rock and roll...now! Find three words of your own. Until recently, a good example of a static category was dry cleaning. Given the increased consumer interest in cleaning up our environment, "non-toxic" cleaners have popped up offering a significant new option for their target consumers.

I have a friend who owns two dry cleaning stores and in recent years has developed a significant home delivery business. I recently suggested he look at what related products he could sell and deliver at the same time. I challenged him to continue innovating and to look for "What's next?" in the dry cleaning category.

Another dormant category is known professionally as JJP. Your great, great, great grandmother invented JJP. No kidding—someone's grandmother did. What's unusual is that while most categories have evolved significantly in the past twenty years, this category has not changed a bit since Granny invented it. It may be in a different jar with a printed label, but the product is identical to that of grannies.

The JJP category I am referring to has been declining in total cases sold per capita for 40 years, and not one player in the category has done anything significant about it. It's as if Granny won't let go. The only change of any note has been what appears to be an undeclared package design competition, albeit one confined to graphics. Unfortunately for the brands competing in the category, this is a competition that has generally gone unnoticed by target consumers.

Consumers are so bored with JJP that they simply keep drifting away. By the way, JJP stands for "Jams, Jellies and Preserves". Let's face it, granny needed to "set up" her preserves in order for the family to have the experience of eating fruit during the winter. Such is no longer the case. As a kid, I remember eating the preserves that my grandmother set up. "Set up" are the words my grandmother used to refer to what we now call canning. Do you know anyone who still cans preserves? Check out the size of the canning category the next time you are in the supermarket—if you can find it at all. I recall the ladies of the canning era as proud of their work to the extent that they always made plenty extra to give away. Additionally, I recall that all the jams tasted basically the same. For the most part that has not changed. They all still taste the same to me, just as they did 50 years ago.

The main problem with the JJP category today is that you can buy fruit and fruity things all over the supermarket and they all taste much more like real fruit than JJP ever did. It's no wonder JJP doesn't taste like real fruit considering it's been literally cooked to death.

Categories evolve constantly and if someone else creates "What's next?" in yours, you will surely be at the receiving end of it. That's painful. Most of the companies that manage secondary brands seem to automatically assume that submissive posture. They simply follow and leave the innovation up to the leading brand. I hope to change your thinking about that.

Having said that, I am compelled to share with you an "innovation" in the JJP category that is simply too insignificant to register meaningful impact.

My expectation for "What's next?" in this, or any category, is a breakthrough—a clear step forward. Here it is. I recently took a close look at the category to see what the participating brands are saying about their JJP. I found: "Legendary Spreadable Fruit," "Since 1897," "Sonoma County Classics," "Produced Without Boiling," "Signature Collection," "An Old French Recipe," "Since 1885," "The Original." To me, none of these statements seem like "What's next?" Chances are, there are a significant number of consumers that are looking for what is next. There are very few looking for what passed.

Being Active Is Critical

Approximately seven years ago, I received an assignment from a client who had three brands in the micro-cup category. Micro-cups are those small, single-serving, shelf-stable microwavable cups that feature food you can heat and eat quickly. The marketing director indicated the need to reposition one of their brands which was, in his word, "floundering." I responded, "Great! We can do that. What about your other two brands?" He said they were fine. Again I asked, "What about the other two?" He repeated that they were fine. Again I asked, "What about the other two?" This time, he was beginning to get irritated but remained polite, and again, replied that they were fine.

This is a classic situation in companies with multiple brands. There are brands that need help and are highlighted for that reason. There are also brands that are identified as having growth potential for a myriad of reasons. Upper management will spend against both of these scenarios. What that leaves are brands that are dormant. In the eyes of management these brands are okay and are to be left alone. For the time being, these dormant brands are left to the assistant brand manager who is expected to maintain them, typically with no funds allocated to the task. They are essentially waiting for something to go wrong and then the attention will come. To my mind, waiting guarantees that something will go wrong. It is critical to keep up a continuous effort to develop and be responsible for "What's next?" You must keep your product or service evolving. If you are the head of marketing and have brand managers reporting to you, I suggest you issue them the following challenge, one that will ensure the longevity of each brand. Simply ask each manager what positioning innovation he/she is going to implement with the brand in the next nine months? It is also a great question to ask yourself.

So, while the "big guys" create dormant categories, many small business categories simply exist as dormant because their participants are ignorant. They simply do not know how to innovate. Again, that's great news for you.

In the mid '70s, one of my clients called me to announce that he was leaving Hunt-Wesson for a marketing position in a smaller company. He was excited to finally be free of the corporate bureaucracy. He said he would be contacting me soon to initiate a project.

I did not hear from him for six months and when I did, he announced that he was out of work and looking for a new job. He said that they hired him to grow the business but refused to give him the funds to do it. I was sympathetic; how could anyone expect to grow a business without spending money? I bought into that logic for a long time, but it's absolutely not true. Crucial positioning innovations—remember, "made from sugar" and "movie theatre butter"—do not have to be expensive. So ask yourself right now: "What positioning innovation am I going to implement on my product or service in the next nine months?" Then nine months later ask yourself again, and every nine months after that. To put the question in layman's terms, "How am I going to re-characterize my product or service on a continuing basis in order to create renewed interest in it?"

A Little Work Now

The key to success lies in defining and communicating a powerful selling proposition directly to your target consumer. Seriously—my clients have held me accountable for creating success and as a result of that responsibility, I have identified a methodology that, if understood and followed, will work for you as well as it does for me. You can assume that everything you read in this book has been developed from a consumer's perspective. Everything I've created has been for the client but on behalf of their target consumer. It represents what the target consumers would have created for themselves had they known how. I am quite sure that consumers do not know how to do this and never will. What target consumers do well is consume; they do not create. Otherwise they'd be referred to as target creators.

I now want you to take the time to do something that will greatly enhance your experience of this book. It involves a little work, but if you want to develop the skill I described in the previous paragraph, it will make a huge difference, I promise. While I created this book to be entertaining and enlightening, it is primarily structured as a learning tool. In this regard, you can either take the million-dollar course by doing a bit of work or simply read on and pick up some very cool terminology. I recommend you go for the million-dollar course that begins with the following exercise.

Page 213 was created for you to write down the answers to seven questions. I ask that you write them down as I talk you through them here. You will be encouraged to revisit this page several times as you read on. In that regard you may want to consider using a pencil with a big fat eraser.

You will answer the questions based upon what you know and, if you are not sure what any of the terminology means, you can guess or leave it blank. I am interested in what you generate here based on your experience to date. Your answers will evolve significantly as you continue reading.

Question 1: What is your product or service?

Question 2: What is the key impact point of your product or service, and what are its secondary impact points, if any? (An impact point is the place where your target consumer is exposed to your product— usually a homepage, a package, a brochure, a storefront or even an ad in the *Yellow Pages*.)

Question 3: What category do you compete in?

Question 4: What is your product's key benefit? (A "benefit" is generally defined as what the target consumer gets out of using your product or service.)

Question 5: What are the key attributes of your product or service? (An "attribute" is generally defined as a product or service characteristic.)

Question 6: Does your product or service have character? (For now, answer the question based on whatever meaning the word "character" has for you.)

Question 7: Do you consider your product remarkable? (This too, is whatever the word "remarkable" means to you at the moment.)

A Bit of Advice

Now, I rarely give advice. In fact, in general my only advice is that you shouldn't take advice. But I'd like to make an exception. My advice is, don't let what you read here become mere knowledge. If you do, it will fade away fast. Knowledge is okay, but it only makes you more intelligent, as in IQ. Intelligence seems to be gauged by the accumulation of knowledge that one can recall. A reasonable amount of knowledge is necessary, but in my experience, the more intelligent people become (i.e., the more information they store), the less effective they are. Increased intelligence causes intellectual conflict and generally leads to indecision. The more intelligent a person is, the less likely he or she will make the shifts in thinking that are needed to impact or improve their business. The same is usually true of their personal lives as well. So if you are an entrepreneur who never got to Harvard and fell short of an MBA, you're in the right place.

Given that we are in the "Information Age", it is now easier for us to become more intelligent than ever before. We are drowning in information. If Aristotle were alive today, his life would serve a very different purpose. He would dump deductive reasoning in favor of inductive reasoning. He would invent a way for us to live with all of this information and function with an awareness that would allow us to be highly effective in spite of it. Inductive reasoning would be a tool for humans to learn how to be naturally aware and thereby more effective. Where do I sign up for that course?

I do not consider myself unusually intelligent. I do consider myself highly aware, however, and I value that as a far more actionable characteristic, particularly in the dynamic world of marketing. Do not discount the value of being aware. A simple word, it is undeservedly unimpressive when compared to "intelligent". We have all been indoctrinated from birth to acquire intelligence; I do not recall ever being taught to acquire awareness. You see, when I'm aware, I'm not at all bound up by an overabundance of knowledge. I have the tools to adjust and adapt appropriately and creatively as circumstances change, which they do—and change, and change, daily. In that regard, I am an opportunist which works well for me. I am into changing things instead of waiting for the change to occur and then analyzing

I did not know what to cut, yet had to figure it out at that moment. I knew that I needed to involve the VP and his team in resetting the presentation context. I quickly read off the section headings and we all agreed on what would be left out. I figured if he took responsibility for what was removed, it would go well. It did go very well and we got another assignment immediately. My giving them the choices set a new context for the presentation, one that they were aligned with. They were listening.

Adapting is not always stressful although it always seems to be unexpected. I will share a once-in-a-life-time experience. It demonstrates that occasionally, miracles actually do happen and that we don't always know exactly what's going on around us. In the early days when I alone was soliciting work, I was very intentional about every aspect of our capabilities pitch. That included prospecting, getting the appointment, giving the pitch and closing the deal. To get started, I sent a box of products that we were responsible for creating to 10 corporate presidents on the West Coast, hoping for the best. These were cold calls as I did not know any of them nor did I have any referrals. My attempts to follow up by phone fell on deaf ears. I was unable to talk to any of the prospects.

Then I received a call that was a classic. The secretary for the president of a major coffee company in San Francisco called to say that her boss had received my package and instructed her to set up a presentation for their entire marketing staff. I was blown away by the apparent effectiveness of my letter. I saw no reason to bring up my prior failed attempt to speak to him on the phone.

A couple of weeks later I arrived at their offices in San Francisco and was greeted warmly by the receptionist who escorted me into a small presentation room. I set up my slide projector and waited—this was long before computers and *Microsoft PowerPoint* presentations. Soon, the room was full. I was with the president, the CEO (his brother), the VP of marketing (his nephew), the VP of operations (his other nephew) and two other marketing people not related to the family. At this point, I recall thinking, "I must be one hell of a letter writer." The president, known simply as Mr. Edward, proceeded to introduce me to his team. After about three minutes,

I realized that the president was under the impression that I was a distant family member, specifically a distant cousin. I must have turned red but I could not think of anything to say at that point that would further my cause, so I said nothing. I smiled, but was careful not to nod, since that, I reasoned, would have been dishonest. When the introductions were over, I did my capabilities presentation. They asked for a proposal, which I gave them and which they approved. We delivered a winner, and to this date, I've never told a soul.

That was only the beginning. Although I rarely saw Mr. Edward, we performed package design services for his company for the next five years until they sold the company. It was not my intention to mislead the family, but for the first several months I could not help but feel guilty about not coming clean. It was at about that time that, in a rare meeting with Mr. Edward, I was introduced to another cousin, a non-family-member cousin. At that moment, I realized Mr. Edward had a habit of referring to people he felt comfortable with as cousins. In that instant, I dropped any guilt associated with that relationship and replaced it with a sense of having become less important.

So, I adapted, became a cousin, then discovered the true meaning of the word and readapted back to my old self.

To this day I remain adaptable—you should too.

The Remarkability Paradigm
Chapter Seven

What Lies Ahead?

What I am about to share with you are a series of distinctions and abstractions that come together to form a paradigm. *Webster* has a couple of definitions for "paradigm". One is: "An example that serves as a pattern or model for something, especially one that forms the basis for a methodology or theory." The other is: "A generally accepted model of how ideas relate to one another forming a conceptual framework within which scientific research is carried out."

From the above definitions, I have developed a hybrid: "A model that allows one to evaluate how ideas relate to one another." The power of my special paradigm lies not in its brilliance but in its origin.

For years, we've had the privilege to be associated with the launching or restaging of a product or service about every three weeks. This has given me a unique vantage point. My team and I are involved with each and every project. We are also the only people I know of on the planet who have that experience routinely. I am sure there are others but I have not met any. So, you see, this paradigm is born out of repetition, exposure and awareness.

One result of all this experience is that I am able to respond to any marketing situation, even those that appear absolutely unique on the surface. Only a short while ago, a client called with a cat litter issue that immediately brought to mind a previous challenge in the toothpaste category. The circumstances were identical and I instantly drew the analogy with the client. In retrospect, that seems a little weird to me now; I wonder if the client thought so, too.

Given my vantage point, it is only natural that I have developed a keen interest in identifying what works and what doesn't. When something significant repeatedly occurs, I declare it a distinction that can be counted on until—

well, until it no longer occurs. In this context, what follows is not only real, but you can absolutely count on it. That's powerful in a world where reality is measured by highly manipulated TV shows.

The Operating State

As we look at the paradigm, it is useful to understand the basic nature of the target consumers we are addressing. They are, first of all, human just like us. As humans, we think in generalities, which have us organizing things into categories. Organizing is one way in which we make life more comfortable. Have you ever noticed what happens when you are alone in a crowd? You're on a subway train or at a cocktail party, and immediately you're assessing everyone you see and placing them in groups that you've already created for the people you meet to fit into. That guy's a jerk, that hot-looking lady's stuck up, etc. You don't even know them, but to deal with them, you have to categorize them. It's what we do. Those guys organizing stuff at the supermarket are just doing what comes naturally. By the way, this categorizing thing almost always manifests itself in cynicism. "What's wrong here?" Sound familiar? I discussed it briefly in the first chapter—humans always look for what is wrong. It's pervasive and, as a marketer, you need to stay present to its effect on your work. In fact, check yourself right now. What is the mind set that you are using as you read this book? Chances are if you have any marketing experience or education of your own, you are looking for what is wrong here with absolutely no prior intention. It is just there.

The operating state of humans is worth getting straight. If you think you are the exception, you are deluding yourself and, operating at a disadvantage. That's because recognizing "What's wrong here?" as your operating state is your only hope of empowerment in both your business and your life.

I discovered many years ago that I was operating that way, and that it was getting in the way of my creativity. Can you see the conflict? If I am always looking for what's wrong, how effective will I be at inventing what is new or next for my clients?

I know many of you pride yourselves on being optimistic. My experience is that optimism will not alter your operating state. "What's wrong here?" is far more powerful and pervasive than you and I trying to be optimistic.

First, I decided I would create something to replace it; something short and easy to remember. It would need to be a few words that would allow me to create freely.

If you were following me on the freeway you may notice that my license plate reads "NU STUFF". I've had that plate for years and initially thought "nu stuff" might work as my new operating state. I tried it for a while, but discovered the nature of it did not challenge me. I also think it's too cute… not serious enough.

As I continued looking, I began to form what turned out to be the perfect operating state for me. It contains absolutely no ego and keeps me on my creative toes 24/7. It's: "What's next?" Yes, "What's next?" from Chapter 6. It works because it has me in a constant inquiry as to what is next? When my creative team presents their work to me, everything presented is fully considered. The creative is never pared down by "What's wrong here?"; it has me always looking to the future, a process that works for me, for my team and, most importantly, for my clients. Looking closely at the nature of the creative world, it is not surprising that an egotistical element creeps in. As one who has operated in that arena (egotism) for a number of years, I can tell you it is a phase that will eventually pass. It has never been a good idea to get too enamored with one's own PR.

One problem that popped up almost immediately was potentially a killer. It was the same force that makes being optimistic almost impossible—I was unable to stay present to my new "What's next?" operating state. As it turns out, "What's wrong here?" has one hell of a strong hold in our subconscious minds. My cure was to create something that would serve as a constant reminder of my new operating state. I did exactly what you would have done; I bought a monkey. More specifically, a stuffed monkey. That monkey sits on a pedestal next to the door in my office and is poised with his right hand in the air. I can't help but give him a high five every time I walk through that door, which happens between 9 or 10 times daily. That high five triggers "What's next?" for me. I am sure, without the monkey, "What's wrong here?" would be on my face like an alien. So…

create a new operating state for yourself; then go get a monkey.

The Paradigm Framework

Given that the paradigm is based on observing the reactions of hundreds of thousands of consumers, it should not come as a surprise that their purchasing habits are formed by normal behavioral patterns.

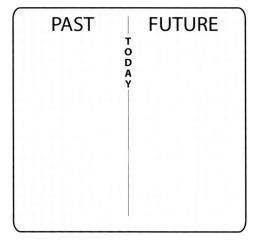

The paradigm is rooted in time and starts with a vertical line in the center, which represents TODAY. The left side of the paradigm represents the PAST and the right side represents the FUTURE.

As marketers, what you and I are stuck with here is that target consumers operate on the left side of the paradigm. In other words, they operate from what they have experienced, which of course, is all in the past. You and I must launch new products or services that must appear to come from the future. This is a fundamental operating characteristic of the marketing world. If we appear on the left side, as others currently do, we are going to struggle.

While the paradigm is expressed in time, it is truly not about time. It's 100% about change—the effect that change has on your product or service, and the end result your product or service has on the change that occurs in your category. Deepak Chopra said there is no such thing as time—that it was made up only to measure change. As it relates to the paradigm, he's right on the mark.

Change is the most dominant factor confronting us in life and, by extension, in marketing. We humans believe that when everything is okay, it's going to stay that way. The only thing you can count on for sure is that life is not ever going to stay the way it is. That is particularly true of the category you are competing in. You need to get into the "change game" and play as if your bank account depends upon it, because it does.

Have you noticed that we spend most of our time arranging our lives with the idea that as soon as we get our lives perfectly arranged, everything will be okay? On that day everything will work and we can take a break from all the arranging. So, we get it arranged and take a break, and then...it changes. And if we stay on our break, we get behind in the game.

What you need then, is a context based on change. You need an operating paradigm that actually thrives on it. What I am distinguishing here is an active marketing paradigm that directly addresses that need.

Looking closer at the left side of the paradigm, both today and the past have a couple of things in common which are important to you and me as marketers. First, they are familiar to our target consumers. Every day, humans encounter new people and new places, yet somehow they are all familiar. Many of them have never seen each other before, yet they are all familiar, and that makes it comfortable. To say it another way, familiarity makes everything okay, and we humans have to make everything okay. The past has already happened so it too, for the most part, is familiar and comfortable.

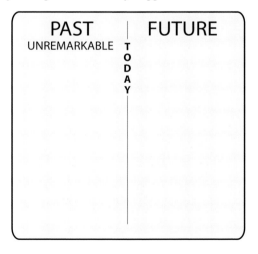

In dealing with this subject, it's helpful to look at it from the consumer's perspective. I'm going to say that the left side of the paradigm, the past, shows up as unremarkable to target consumers. Unremarkable is simply the word I've chosen for the purpose of this discussion. Do not look it up in the dictionary.

We define "unremarkable" as familiar and comfortable—the way your category currently exists for your target consumer. Unremarkable isn't bad, per se, it's just the way the category is now. Make sure you understand that—unremarkable is not bad, it merely distinguishes the way things in your category are currently perceived by your target consumer.

If the left side of the paradigm appears unremarkable to target consumers, then what about the right side—the future? It shows up for your target consumer as remarkable—as a breakthrough in your category.

You could say that life comes at us from the future. That is, it comes at us from the right side of the paradigm to the left. Over time, we have conditioned ourselves to watch for it. We are creatures who, for whatever reason, are interested in "What's next?" As you might expect, society has conveniently arranged itself around this behavioral pattern…by selling us news. News is no accident; we demand it and they provide it. You can watch it, you can read it and you can find it everywhere. If they consider it remarkable, they will interrupt your life and get it to you as fast as they can. That's "breaking news". Breaking news, I have discovered, is everything from airplanes flying into a building to a fender bender on the expressway. Accidents are the news industry's default story on a slow news day, and they know that you and I stop to listen every time.

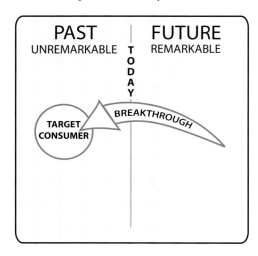

Marketers often refer to a breakthrough as a "WOW". A breakthrough is caused when two things occur for the target consumer upon initial contact. One, their attention is grabbed in a remarkable way, and two, your selling proposition is immediately perceived as remarkable. All of that occurs at the impact point—your homepage, your pop up ad, a package, brochure, a flyer, commercial—whatever your initial impact point happens to be.

The initial perception of uniqueness communicates that your product or service is an alternative to all other products or services in the category. That causes the target consumer to engage. Typically, this is accomplished by creating a unique graphic presentation for your product or service. It serves to highlight the entry point for your target consumer to engage in your selling proposition. It does not matter if it's a TV commercial, a consumer product package or an ad in the *Yellow Pages*. If the presentation is unique, the message communicated prior to the target consumer reading any copy or hearing any spoken message is that your product or service is an alternative within the category. If that happens, they will engage in your selling proposition.

The immediate communication of your remarkable selling proposition completes that consumer "WOW" that marketers are always looking for. It is that initial bit of information that cuts straight to your target consumer's benefit and validates it. A purchase results unless the target consumer considers the product or service inappropriate for them. I will show you exactly how this is done.

We declare that anything currently exposed to the target consumer (the left side) is distinguished as unremarkable. It is therefore familiar and comfortable to the target consumer, and not likely to cause a reaction. Conversely, anything newly exposed to the target consumer that causes them to engage in the selling proposition is considered remarkable. That consumer engagement triggers everything.

Now is a great time to look at your initial response to question seven on page 213 and see if you want to change your mind. In this context, do you consider your product or service unremarkable or remarkable? Think about it for a moment. I recommend you not read further until you understand that your product or service is unremarkable. Remember—unremarkable is anything currently in your category that your target consumer is familiar with. This is merely a declaration so we can deal with it within the context of the paradigm.

The paradigm presumes that target consumers do not respond to selling propositions they perceive as unremarkable and, by definition, do respond to selling propositions they perceive as remarkable. Your target consumer's perception of "remarkability" thereby becomes your objective.

I have observed that there are two opportunities to be perceived as remarkable (note the word "perceived"). In this conversation we are only dealing with the perception of the target consumers—not your perception, not mine, only theirs.

Product/Service vs. Selling Proposition

The first opportunity to be perceived as remarkable by your target consumer is in your product or service. A number of years ago, while working with a brand team, the idea of putting granola on top of yogurt emerged. It was assumed that as people moved down the supermarket aisle and encountered the yogurt section, they would stop and engage.

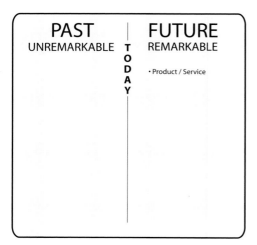

Granola on top of yogurt occurred as a breakthrough in the yogurt category. That's how remarkability occurs for the target consumer, as a breakthrough in an established category. On that day, consumers were exposed to that selling proposition, and those who considered it to be appropriate purchased it.

This area of remarkable product or service is where most companies think the big opportunities lie. Not true at all.

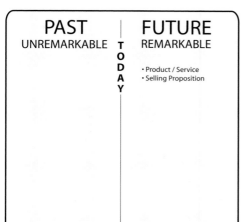

The second opportunity to be perceived as remarkable is in the area of your selling proposition. While the two are extremely integrated, it is of value to pull them apart, as we will do here in order to evaluate the power of each on its own merits.

The nature of the selling proposition is such that it is possible to launch a new business that is absolutely unremarkable if it is empowered with a remarkable selling proposition. However, if you launch a remarkable business with an unremarkable selling proposition, you will suffer at the very least and likely fail. This is why I like to say the "keys to the vault" are in the selling proposition…your remarkable selling proposition.

The Importance of Triggers

I can summarize the goal of marketing as having your product perceived as remarkable by your target consumer on an ongoing basis. This is correct, but it can be misleading in terms of how best to accomplish it.

Just as the mind tends to think in generalities, marketers have treated products and services and their selling propositions as whole and complete entities. In fact, that is how they are validated in research—as whole and complete concepts. There's nothing wrong with that, but I offer a more powerful approach when creating a remarkable selling proposition for your product or service.

Over time, we have discovered that target consumers are "triggered" to engage in a product's selling proposition and prompted to make the purchase. That is to say a specific element or several elements of the selling proposition cause consumers to engage in the complete selling proposition. A trigger can be either written or spoken words, graphics or even structure. You will recall the words "made from sugar" in the *Splenda* example. That particular element is a product attribute. That particular characteristic of the product triggered a favorable target consumer response that led to millions of dollars in sales.

Can you imagine the power of being able to identify two or three triggers that specifically cause your target consumer to engage in your selling proposition? That's the power of having the "WOW" that all marketers are looking for. As you work with this book, you will deconstruct your selling proposition into its fundamental elements and pursue multiple remarkable triggers within each element.

My experience is that you can go to war with just one remarkable trigger. We have developed and validated as many as five within one selling proposition, but that's rare. Two or three will do the job very well. So, overall, remarkability is achieved through the development and incorporation of several remarkable triggers into your selling proposition.

Dealing with "Pull"

You will remember the past is where humans are familiar and comfortable, and it is where they hang out. In fact, we have noticed that all people have

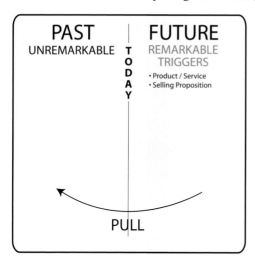

an affinity for the left side of the paradigm. They are not comfortable dealing with the future. The future is unknown; it's mysterious and extremely uncomfortable and "What's next?" comes relentlessly at them from the future. They are forced to deal with "What's next?" daily.

Given that consumers have no choice in the matter of new stuff coming at them from the future, they have learned to expect it and now engage it automatically. We humans, as it turns out, are hard-wired to pull any-thing that comes at us from the future back into the past and to do it as fast as we can. That is to say hard-wired in the brain meaning we have no say in the matter. Not one of us can control that. You could say that "pull" is how we make everything okay. It's how we deal with all things that show up as exciting, whether good or bad. It appears to be a defense mechanism that somehow protects us, a method operating on the level of target consumers making purchase decisions.

Thinking back to the "granola on top of yogurt" example, I am reminded that few new products or services are proprietary and, therefore, are routinely copied or eclipsed by the competition. Granola on top of yogurt was only the beginning of that particular craze. Soon there were sprinkles, fruit bits, *Snickers* bits, etc. Can you see how fast target consumers pulled that one to the left side of the paradigm?

We have come to an important juncture because understanding that your business is unremarkable is your access to inventing remarkability. If you are stuck thinking that your current business is remarkable, I invite you to review my definition of "unremarkable": the way your product or service currently occurs to your target consumer. They are familiar with it...yes?

By the way, do not confuse unique with remarkable. Your product may well be unique. But if your selling proposition has been in your category (just as it is now) even for a short time, your target consumer will have pulled it back to the left side of the paradigm. It doesn't take long—about the same amount of time it took you to get familiar with your last new car.

Remember the first day you got the car and how it made you feel when driving it? You were so careful with it, and careful about parking it. And now? You still have the car, but what happened to the feeling? Your car is in your garage with several dents and scratches, and that doesn't seem to bother you. You cannot maintain those feelings. Humans are hard-wired to make everything comfortable, they can't help that. Not them, or you.

Remember your first day in a new job; the excitement, anticipation, fear. Now, how do you feel about your job? Relationships, too. Remember the first date? Remember those feelings? Sorry, that's just the way it is. It doesn't matter if the news is good or bad—we pull it back. Remember 9/11 and how badly you needed to make it okay, to make it comfortable? What all of this means is that when you and I launch something remarkable it cannot remain so.

Do you understand my point? I'm talking about you being a more effective marketer simply by being aware of two pervasive human characteristics. I am referring to "pull" and now adding to it "What's next?" Don't make the mistake of thinking that these characteristics only apply to target consumers. There is a distinct advantage in understanding how they affect your target consumers, but you must also understand how they affect you. Do you see that these two distinctions affect how you process the information I'm sharing with you right now? My advice is that you remain aware.

So how do you feel about "pull"? Bad news? Good news? Think about how it would be if it were not there. What is it actually doing? Let's say that pull did not exist for a moment. Let's say you are an institutional detergent manufacturer and have just invented a technology that performs on a whole new level. A level that significantly outperforms *Tide*. You pitch it to the trade and they respond by saying, "Sorry, but the category is full of remarkable products right now. As soon as consumers pull one of our current products over to the left side of the paradigm, we'll consider yours. We're just waiting for the products we currently have to become unremarkable."

So, you see, "pull" is your friend. It does not discriminate. It in no way favors the big guy any more than it favors you. It creates a level playing field. It is constantly creating a clearing for remarkability to show up, remarkability that you can create just as well as the next guy. For the most part, in the world of small and medium-size businesses, there is no awareness of this distinction… good news for you again.

Target consumers are rather confused about this. If you ask them, they will trick you because they don't distinguish the present from the future. If you get a group of them in a room and ask them to create the next-generation TV show, they will create *Desperate Housewives* and swear to you that it's part of the future. They won't even recognize it as having already been done.

The Power of Character

Given that we are aggressively in pursuit of remarkable triggers, it is critical that we have a context for creating them. It took me six years to discover the difference between unremarkable and remarkable as it impacts the target consumer. One way to view it is by asking the following: What do you have to do to an unremarkable element on the left side of the paradigm that will move it to the right side and have it become remarkable? The day I discovered the answer to that, I felt I had cracked the *Da Vinci Code*. I had, in fact, cracked the "Remarkability Code" which has proven far less mysterious than that *Da Vinci* thing, yet far more important in my life. As it turns out, like most great insights, it is fairly simple.

My team had long been scrutinizing elements that I personally thought were triggering target consumers looking for a common theme. After far longer than I want to admit, we noticed that successful products and services all shared characteristics that seemed new to the category. They simply seemed fresher than most of the other elements out there. The next thing we observed was that they were also more interesting. Finally, we recognized that these characteristics caused us to feel better about the product, i.e., friendlier towards it. We felt the product was more "credible" than its competition. We actually felt it was special and noticed that we began to develop an affinity and loyalty towards it. We perceived that we were referring it to others we thought it appropriate for.

In time, I realized we were reacting much as we would to a human being. Bingo! It was at that point that I figured it out. I looked closely at my friends and assessed what they all had in common. They are an eclectic bunch whom I find interesting. In fact, I frequently refer to them as a cast of characters, and they are exactly that. There it was—the answer.

It is only one thing. If you add it to anything currently perceived as unremarkable by your target consumer, it will absolutely move it to the remarkable side of the paradigm.

It's CHARACTER.

It's not perfect, but it's the closest word I can find. Therefore, "character", for this purpose, needs to be clearly defined. Here, too, I am simply declaring what I mean by character. I am not referring to Mickey Mouse or Jack Nicholson. The character I'm referring to is more specific than that. *Webster* defines it

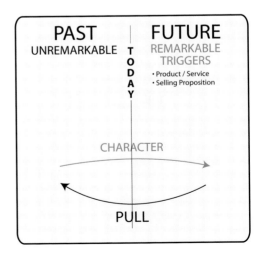

very well as "qualities that make something interesting." I say that "character" includes words, graphics and even physical materials such as a uniquely unexpected container for potato chips or that giant "boot car" I showed you awhile back. These things have character that directly impresses the target consumer as interesting. Let me say that again, for it is critical that you get this. "Character" is anything, be it a graphic, a word or something physical in nature that the target will relate to or have an affinity for when it is exposed to the target as one of your positioning elements. How much character is there in your current selling proposition? Here is a great example.

You can bet that somewhere in the files at *General Mills* there are old research findings that clearly indicate that you cannot sell yogurt to kids. That is the way it used to be. When they asked moms, they were told that their kids said it was too bitter. When they asked kids, they were told, "No thanks, my mom eats yogurt. Not for me."

They simply added character to the delivery system by putting it into plastic tubes. They gave it a sub-brand name with character: *Go-Gurt*. Notice it is not necessary to define the product in its name but merely to characterize it. What is it? Yogurt. No. They added character there, too. The generic descriptor became "portable yogurt". There was no such thing as portable yogurt then. The key graphics show a heavily characterized kid on his BMX enjoying the product. Character is appropriately distributed throughout the selling proposition. The remarkability is therefore distributed evenly throughout the selling proposition as well. This is a great example of multiple remarkable

triggers within one selling proposition, all driven by added character. This is also a great time to observe that none of *Go-Gurt*'s technology is proprietary, yet it would be difficult to duplicate its positioning elements without infringing upon its copyright.

Now for the bad news. Just as I observed earlier, *Go-Gurt* was absolutely remarkable at its launch but now…not at all. Even your supermarket private label brand has yogurt in plastic tubes.

Be sure that as you add character in pursuit of remarkability, you understand what you are doing. Remember, this paradigm is not time based and that it's rooted in change. What you are doing is illustrated by the nature of the character arrow in the paradigm diagram. You are initiating change in your category and your competition will suffer for it.

Now that you understand the power of character, turn your attention once again to page 213 and review question number six. It is likely that you now have an idea about how to improve in this area.

The Truing Principle

Can you see that the paradigm is almost complete? If you think about it, it's easy to add character and make a positioning element remarkable. There is, however, a truing principle that makes it much more of a challenge. The character you add must also be appropriate.

That is, appropriate in the eyes of the target consumer.

If you are a basketball fan or just mildly aware of the sport, you will appreciate the following analogy.

In the NBA, who are the most remarkable players? Michael Jordan,

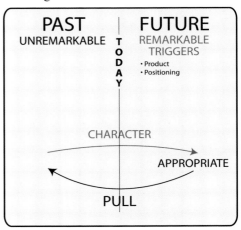

Shaquille O'Neal, Kobe Bryant and Magic Johnson are some who are considered the most remarkable. And what makes them so? I am going to say they are the most remarkable and consequently the highest paid because they have the most character. Consider for a moment the difference between Michael Jordan and Tim Duncan. Both are MVPs and both won championships but who sold the most jerseys? It was Michael Jordan by far. Exciting to watch his basketball skills and interesting to watch his smile and follow his personal life. That's character—personal characteristics that his target consumers (fans) developed a relationship with.

At the end of the 1998 NBA season, there was one player who had won Defensive Player of the Year twice and led the NBA in rebounds per game seven years in a row, yet few people paid attention. He was perceived as absolutely unremarkable. Beyond his own team he was virtually unknown.

Then, one night, he showed up on the court with half his hair dyed green and the other half dyed orange. On that night, at that game, Dennis Rodman moved from the left side of the paradigm to the right. He went from being perceived as unremarkable to being perceived as remarkable by millions of basketball fans across the country. He did it simply by adding character. He changed his hair from black to green and orange and suddenly, he went from no endorsements to *Carl's Jr.* I am positive Rodman knew exactly what he was doing; his new hair-do was apparently considered appropriate by the target, otherwise, there would have been no *Carl's Jr.* commercials.

Then one day, while at a book signing, Rodman showed up in a wedding dress. Photographs of the incident were immediately published in all the tabloids. Suddenly he was no longer considered appropriate by the target, and, therefore, no more *Carl's Jr.* contract.

Recall your last job interview. If you showed up on the left side of the paradigm, in the past, you did not get the job. If you showed up on the right side, in the future, remarkable and appropriate, I guarantee you got the job. In the middle, the in-between area, I cannot say. Think about it; it applies anywhere you are selling anything, including yourself…especially yourself. Selling yourself is ongoing: a simple presentation to your boss, a proposal of marriage…left side, you remain single, right side, you can start working on your family.

I know of only three examples of inappropriate selling propositions and it was not until circumstances changed over time that they became so. The first occurred back in the late '70s when we were hired to work on a diet product being nationally distributed. It was generically referred to as a "diet plan candy". The product was experiencing success but had been given to a lady marketer I would describe as aggressive. I will always remember that she had the strongest positive reaction to our creative work I have ever experienced and likely ever will. The initial creative presentation went on for about 20 minutes. When I had finished, all of us were waiting for her reaction. I was unsure and a bit nervous. She was one of those executives who wanted everyone in the room to comment ahead of her. As it went on, I got uneasier. When she finally spoke, she was crystal clear. Her exact words were, "This is the first time I have been able to get excited about this f---ing project"! Then she smiled. (I have not seen this woman in more than 20 years, but I will never forget her words. In the creative world, when you get an accolade, you savor it!)

The recommended changes were incorporated almost immediately. The result was that the product prospered. It was several years later, in mid-1985, the brand name suddenly became incredibly inappropriate. The brand was Ayds Diet Plan candy. Can you imagine the dilemma when the marketing team was faced with the appearance of AIDS, one of the most deadly diseases in modern time? I was no longer working on the brand at that time, but I couldn't help but notice its decline into obscurity over the next few years.

A second example also occurred in the '70s, when Procter & Gamble made a simple package design change to their *Ivory Snow* laundry soap. It exuded the perfect image of family values well before family values became a cliché. In what was characterized as a simple upgrade of their package design, the *Ivory Snow* brand team developed the illustration you see here. What could be more appropriate than a mother and child bonding? The lady in the picture was a 17-year-old model perfect for the desired image. The message here is if you use *Ivory Snow*, your baby will like you.

The illustration is an accurate reproduction of a photograph. The close-up reveals the baby and is cropped tightly on the mother's face to communicate the maximum emotional impact.

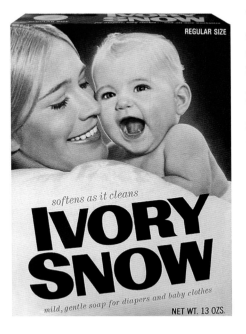

The problem here turned out to be the selection of the model. The lady you see here completed her first of many films in 1972, two years after she began to appear on the front panel of the box. Her name is Marilyn Chambers, no relation that I know of, and the movie was *Behind The Green Door*. That movie launched her career as a major porn star. Now, what could be less appropriate? I grabbed this box as Procter & Gamble was aggressively pulling them off the shelves.

The third example took place in an era much different from our own. In 1897, Lever Brothers launched their Gold Dust washing powder across the nation and it was an immediate success. The two characters on the front of the package became known as the Gold Dust Twins and were one of the most well known trademarks of the 19th cen-

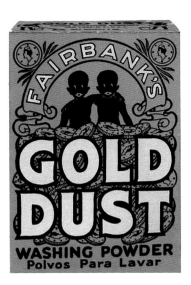

tury. The brand folded in the 1930s for reasons unknown to me. You can clearly see how inappropriate it would be today. I find it incredible that, even at that time, what you see here was a successful brand. What that means is that its selling proposition was considered valid and was accepted by its target consumers as appropriate. I prefer to think it was simply mass ignorance.

More On Remarkability
Chapter Eight

We have now come to an important juncture because understanding that your product or service is unremarkable is your access to inventing remarkability. If you are stuck in believing in the current remarkability of your product or service, you are beating a dead horse.

Remarkability Before the Paradigm

While the paradigm is a relatively new part of my work the distinction "remarkability" has been in my life for a long time. Before the paradigm, remarkability was presented to our clients as a goal to strive for. It characterized the value of separating your product or service from all others in your category. It was a way to distinguish the value of having your product or service be the category alternative. That, in turn, forces target consumers to constantly consider your selling proposition so that every time they make a purchase in your category, whether they buy your product/service or not, they are always considering and reconsidering your product/service as an option. That was a powerful goal even before we identified remarkability's place within the paradigm.

The Origin of Remarkability

This idea of setting yourself apart from others in order to be chosen is one I have carried around for many years. Have you ever noticed that, when you have an insight, the genesis of it is always an occurrence or a lesson that occurred well before? That was my experience with remarkability.

When I was young, I had what is now commonly referred to as a learning disability. It was not severe, but it did mean that reading and writing skills developed slowly for me. I only recognized it in myself when it was diagnosed as an issue for both of my sons.

As a student, I recall that teachers generally did not call on me to respond in class and I certainly did not make myself conspicuous. I was behind in all my classes because it would take me twice as long to read as the other kids and I would only comprehend about half the information. That meant I had to read everything at least twice, which I hated. Most of my assignments simply did not get read. I tried to compensate by paying attention in class, and that's essentially, how I learned. I kept a low profile and as a result I was never the chosen one. I can see now that I made sure I did not stand out as a student. That was my category—"student"—and I survived by being unremarkable in my category. Until eleventh grade, I don't recall ever being chosen for anything academic. I was a master of hiding out in plain sight.

As that school year came to a close, I was summoned to the front office to meet with the principal, Mr. Page. Walking to his office I reviewed all the shady things I had done that week wondering which one he'd caught on to. There were clearly a number of possibilities for him to consider. Once in his office, he initiated a conversation that altered my perception of myself for the rest of my life.

Mr. Page seemed very formal that day. He began the conversation by simply asking me how school was going. I replied "Fine," but in truth I was squeaking by with barely passing grades. I was sure he knew that already. He proceeded to explain that every summer in Columbus, Ohio, there was a two-week government camp and he had chosen me to go as the student representative of the school. I was stunned that he had picked me and had to hold myself back from asking why. He had to know my grades were below average. Instead, I simply thanked him and said I would like to go but would have to check with my parents.

That night, I did not ask my parents; in fact, I never told them about the offer. As flattered as I was, I was terrified that if I went I would be asked to perform intellectually, and would be embarrassed. There was no way I wanted to subject myself to an intellectual environment like that.

The next day, I went back to Mr. Page's office to give him my response. I knew I had to make up something that he would believe and not call my parents to verify. I told him that my parents needed me to work in the summer as a caddy to earn money to buy my school clothes. He seemed to buy that and politely dismissed me. For the next week or so I was afraid he would try to resolve the money issue for me, but when he announced that another student had been picked I knew it was over. I do not recall ever telling anyone, not even my closest friends, about his offer.

Looking back, I now see that it worked out perfectly. I would have been miserable at that camp. On the other hand, just being selected to go gave me the confidence that the learning disability I was experiencing was not an accurate reflection of my intelligence. On that day, I was "the chosen one" and that was enough to make a difference; the only reason Mr. Page could have chosen me was that he somehow perceived me as remarkable. After that experience, I began to look at myself differently. Up until then, my career goal was to go to New York and get a job driving a limousine for some rich dude. I myself take a limousine now and then, and you can be sure I'm always reminded of that old career goal. In retrospect, I suspect Mr. Page knew he was offering me more than a trip to Columbus. At that time I had no idea why he selected me, but for the first time in my life someone considered me to be a remarkable person and that was all that mattered. In retrospect, I think he was more interested in selecting a kid who would be empowered by the experience instead of an "A" student who would be rewarded. If so, his strategy worked for me without my ever leaving town.

Character and Loyalty

Character is what drives remarkability. Character also has a second feature almost equally important. Most marketers strive for the target to develop loyalty to their products or services. What I can tell you for sure is that what you commonly refer to as loyalty is completely and totally driven by character. Character is what the target is loyal to, what they relate to. No character, no loyalty. It is the character driven subject matter that gives target consumers something to be loyal to.

The supermarkets developed "Plain Wrap", the black-and-white packaging that appeared briefly in the late '70s? It was inspired by the slow economy and was the supermarket industry's answer for how to save money. Theoretically it cost less to produce the cheap packaging and the cost savings was to be passed on to the consumer. It had zero character and, in turn, zero loyalty. It was 100% price-driven. A black and white package with no photograph has no character for the consumer to relate to. That lack of character had a second effect that supermarkets did not anticipate. It soon became un-cool to be seen with it in your shopping cart. Once retail supermarkets discovered "Plain Wrap" was reducing their profits, they ended it and no one missed it. As one who was involved in it, I can tell you that there was little cost savings simply by printing the package in two colors instead of four.

Few marketers look to loyalty for profits, but I can tell you that loyalty is what makes profit possible. If a competitive product or service is cheaper than yours, loyalty is the only thing that will hold your target consumer. If you dig into that loyalty, you will discover it is driven by character.

Now that we have agreed on the importance of loyalty, I am going to pull the rug out from under you. Ready? You may recall that when I first referred to loyalty, I phrased it as "what you commonly refer to as loyalty". The truth is there is no loyalty in the realm of marketing; no consumers are ever faithful. What most people call loyalty isn't; it is merely sustained interest. You see, loyalty is defined as "a feeling of devoted attachment" which implies that if things aren't right, your target consumers will hang in. Not so. They will bail out in a heartbeat. Ask the folks at *Equal* about loyalty. Remember how easily their consumers defected to *Splenda* over those three simple words "made from sugar?" *Equal* did not change its product or positioning but the mere perception that something was wrong with and the others in the category caused consumers to abandon those products en masse.

If your consumer gets the impression that things are better over there with a competitive product or service, they will bail. And it is just as true that if they perceive things to be better with your product or service, they will buy it. It is their interest you want—preferably their sustained interest—once you have gotten their attention with remarkable triggers. Want to succeed? Then take my advice and forget what you know about loyalty and instead solicit the sustained interest of your target consumers. And take note of the word "sustained". It implies that you are ever in action creating continuous remarkability because you know now that remarkability, by its intrinsic nature, cannot last.

Does *Tide* really have loyalty or is the brand constantly changing—adding character—in order to sustain the interest of its target consumers? The answer is the latter.

If you want to secure your product or service's future, add character. After you've done so, add more character. Then take a well-deserved short vacation before coming back and adding some more. You will drive your competition nuts.

Character and Profits

One more thing about the value of character—it's the only thing we know of that breeds loyalty, and loyalty is directly related to profit.

Many marketers will be surprised by that statement, but it's true. In most cases, it is easier to increase profit by augmenting character than by any other traditional means. Most of the other moves to increase profit are risky. You can always raise the price of your product or service; you can downgrade its quality; you can also decrease its size. I have seen all these attempts backfire on clients many times. These moves are typically driven by a short-term management edict to show increased profits for the annual financial statements. That scenario should sound familiar if you are a corporate type.

Look back for a second at the paradigm. Remember I said there are only two areas—product/service and selling proposition—in which to be perceived as remarkable? My experience is that there are far more opportunities to be remarkable in the domain of selling proposition than in the domain of product/service. You do not have to launch a new product or service to control your category. I say again, controlling your category does not have to be an expensive proposition. If you are continuously and actively upgrading your selling proposition by adding remarkable triggers, you will control your category, and the only thing your competitors will be able to do is react.

Category Evolution and Natural Selection

You should take a moment to look at where you are playing in the paradigm. Playing in the past is the status quo; playing in the future is where anything is possible. The entire paradigm represents evolution and the natural selection of marketing. If Darwin were alive today, he'd be one hell of a marketer. It's easy to see the evolution in this—it is a function of the pull that forces all new product or service innovations to the unremarkable side of the paradigm. That action creates an opening to be filled on the right side of the paradigm. Given that new entries on the right side are remarkable by definition, evolution is the result. Can you also see the "natural selection"? How about "survival of the fittest"? In this case, you need not be Goliath to survive. In fact, better to be David with his slingshot—character.

If you hang out in the past, you are guaranteed to be at the mercy of others. Hanging out in the future, you are the "cause" in your category and you need not be the category leader. You also do not need to have a significant advertising budget to support your position. You are causing "What's next?" at your impact point, and others are forced to react to you. They suffer, you prosper.

You now know what you need to do in order to succeed. You must be perceived as remarkable by the target...remarkable and appropriate, that is. If so, they will engage and, if you have a valid selling proposition, you will be successful.

The Communications Model
Chapter Nine

You may notice that this is the longest chapter in the book, much lengthier than the others. There's a reason for that: the communications model has many components, but it must be considered as a whole. Therefore, rather than break up this discussion into multiple chapters, I've made it just one to emphasize the importance of understanding that each and every part of the model is important, and that all of the components together contribute to the power of your selling proposition.

One way to understand the communications model is to look at it relative to your sales message (selling proposition). If you made a list of everything you would include in your sales message, it would all fit into one element or another of the communications model. We have identified all of the possible elements and listed them to make it easy to break down your sales message and evaluate it element by element.

Together the remarkability paradigm and the communications model are living systems that represent the two critical tools you will use routinely to create success. Having created both, I can tell you that we refer to them on a daily basis, never trusting that our general knowledge of each is enough to ensure full access to all that is possible. In other words, they are used much in the same way great pilots use a checklist when flying a combat mission. I can assure you, it's extremely dangerous not to refer to your checklist. On pages 211 and 212, I have provided both for easy reference.

Your selling proposition is simply an orchestrated sales message. It's made up of the communications elements that are critical to selling your product or service. You will notice that 15 elements make up the total communications model. Each represents an opportunity to add remarkability to your business message, and thus, experience success.

COMMUNICATIONS MODEL

POSITIONING ELEMENTS

1. **BRAND**
2. **SUB-BRAND**
3. **GENERIC DESCRIPTOR**
4. **SEGMENTS** (Product Groups)
5. **BENEFIT/KEY FEATURE**
   - W.T.B. Why To Buy
   - C.T.A. Call To Action
6. **ATTRIBUTES: (R.T.B.)**
   - Physical
   - Performance
   - Negative
7. **TAG LINE**
8. **ENDORSEMENTS**
9. **KEY GRAPHIC**
10. **GRAPHIC PRESENTATION**
11. **IMPACT**
12. **PRODUCT CONFIGURATION**
13. **CONTAINER CONFIGURATION**
14. **PRODUCT PRESENTATION**
15. **DELIVERY SYSTEM**

Note: Together, the above Positioning Elements make up your Selling Proposition

As I suggested earlier, the communications model you see here has been developed much in the same way as the paradigm—through a long series of observations. In this case, it is from observing many of America's most successful marketers as they brief us on conditions in their respective categories. I live and work with these positioning elements daily. It has been at least five years since we have made any changes to the list of elements and since then it has withstood the test of routine exposure to well over a hundred marketers. Given that level of scrutiny, I am confident that the communications model covers the complete range of possibilities in any selling proposition. The model has been created specifically for use in exploring the development of remarkable triggers. Ultimately, you will create a remarkable selling proposition for your business by working through all of the elements that are appropriate to your business. Having done so, you will identify a series of remarkable triggers that you will assemble into your remarkable selling proposition.

As the communications model reveals, effective marketers break down the overall selling proposition into its positioning elements. It is displayed here so you can follow along with me as I distinguish each of them. You can check each against what you are currently doing in order to gain insight into creating remarkability for your business. As observations occur, flip to page 213 and make note of them.

I will distinguish each of the positioning elements, although keep in mind that it's rare that all are applicable to any given product or service. Those that offer the greatest opportunity for your product or service will become obvious to you as I distinguish them. I recommend you check off the box next to those elements of interest to you on page 213.

Naming Possibilities

There are three naming opportunities to be considered when working on a brand image. They are the company name, the brand name and the sub-brand name. You may have one, two or all three to consider.

I have created a hypothetical dry cleaning business scenario that's based on that of a friend. I will demonstrate three different ways that it could be set up, and how the naming of each would be handled. Let's assume the storefront is its key impact point for this company that has five stores. In addition to the face and display windows, it has a sign on a pole. We will only consider the sign for this demonstration.

1) In the first scenario, this hypothetical company's name also functions as its brand name for all five stores. That means the name "Carriage Trade" will appear on all of the business forms as well as the branded areas such as the store front, the website, the *Yellow Pages* ad and so on.

NAME   SIGN

Company/Brand: Carriage Trade

2) In the second scenario, the hypothetical company name also functions as the brand name for only four of the five stores. The fifth store is located close to the airport and specializes in thirty-minute pickup and delivery. To accommodate the special nature of this store, the word "Express" has been added as a sub-brand. That means the name Carriage Trade will appear on the business forms and the name "Carriage Trade Express" will appear on all the branded areas like store front, the website, the *Yellow Pages* ad and so on.

NAME   SIGN

Company/Brand: Carriage Trade

Sub-Brand: Express

3) In the third scenario, a hypothetical company, called California Cleaning bought Carriage Trade. This name does not function as the brand nor sub-brand because the company has several businesses, only one of which is dry cleaning. The company name may be applied to the business forms but will not appear on any of the branded materials. The parent company, California Cleaning is irrelevant to

the marketing of the cleaning business. The brand and sub-brand will appear on all the branded areas like the storefront, the website, the *Yellow Pages* ad and so on.

NAME   SIGN

Company: California Cleaning

Brand: Carriage Trade

Sub-Brand: Express

The Generic Descriptor

You will want to locate your generic descriptor directly under the brand or sub-brand name to qualify it. You will recall that the function of a brand or sub-brand is to characterize, not to define the product. That means it needs to be quickly qualified. The generic descriptor accurately defines the product so that when the target consumer encounters both together, a complete communication is accomplished. The best of all scenarios is when the brand and generic descriptor are so tightly designed together they are perceived as one graphic unit. This is executed to perfection on the *Splenda* package that follows.

Marketers typically look to the generic descriptor last for an opportunity to create remarkability, yet when it works it can be deadly. It occurs particularly powerful for target consumers because they so rarely encounter a generic descriptor that way. When they do, it is usually perceived by target consumers as "new news". New news is what every marketer lives for. When it becomes that important, the smart thing to do is to elevate its prominence.

There are two circumstances when the generic descriptor should be elevated in importance. In both instances this occurs when, in addition to defining the product, significant remarkability is present.

The first circumstance occurs when the new product is configured in such a way as to be considered remarkable by consumers when simply defined. In that case, not elevating it in prominence would be a mistake. It remains, generic by its very nature, and therefore cannot be protected—

that is, you can't own it. The smart marketer distinguishes it by elevating it and adding graphic character to it such as in the case of the General Mills Milk 'n Cereal Bars shown here. Once elevated, we consider it a key feature worthy of just as much prominence as a benefit. The words are generic but their meaning is remarkable. There was no such thing as Milk 'n Cereal Bars at its time of introduction.

You can own the graphic design character that you bring to the words, and that is significant. The courts will allow the competition to copy your product but will not allow them to copy your design. The application of the law in such cases deems that the target consumer not be confused by similarities in appearance.

The second circumstance occurs when you are fortunate enough to add one or two words to the otherwise generic descriptor such that it becomes remarkable. At this point we distinguish it as a tag line that performs the defining task of the generic descriptor.

A good example is the *Pharmaca* chain of pharmacies that has accomplished remarkability by simply adding one word to their generic descriptor. "Integrative Pharmacy" is now a tag line characterizing their pharmacy as remarkable in a world full of traditional pharmacies. It also functions nicely as their generic descriptor. It works in that prospective customers know it is a pharmacy and are triggered to find out the meaning of "integrative". As it turns out, what they meant by integrative is that as you shop, you will find traditional brands right alongside the alternative health or homeopathic options (for instance, *Crest* is next to *Tom's of Maine*).

Now that you are familiar with characterizing generic descriptors so that they empower the selling proposition, I will share with you one generic descriptor that killed a great product. In the late '70s, I was given a package design assignment by the Foremost Dairy Company in San Francisco. At that time there was a very popular no-fat product called IMO in the dairy section. It was not a dairy product but was used as a no-fat substitute for sour cream. Its generic descriptor was "imitation sour cream", selected by its manufacturer as the most effective way to communicate the product. Given that IMO was not a dairy product, it was not subject to strict dairy regulations.

The new product we were given to work on was a dairy product that was very low in fat and tasted very well. It, however, did not qualify as a sour cream product. It was a new product that had to be given a new and appropriate designation by the dairy board. They came up with "reduced-calorie cultured product". I had to put that prominently on the package in lettering half the size of the product name. To this day, I don't remember the name we gave the product but I'll never forget the generic descriptor we were strapped with. The client launched a billboard campaign to introduce it and one billboard was located across from my Wilshire Boulevard office in Santa Monica. I got to look at a huge reproduction of the reduced-calorie cultured product every day. The product failed in a matter of months, so we did not suffer long.

The Brand

Notice on the communications model that "brand" is the first on the list. Brands are rarely remarkable, and if they are, its only immediately after their introduction. In this regard, the brand stands out among all of the other positioning elements. If your brand is established, then it is unremarkable by definition and that's okay. Its long-term function is not remarkability.

As we continue, you will discover that in order to maintain remarkability in your selling proposition you must be willing to seek change in any of the remaining positioning elements on a continuing basis. Considering that the brand is the device by which your product or service is identified, you would not want to change it even if you thought you could achieve remarkability by doing so; that is simply not part of its basic function.

CHARACTERIZING
SHORT
POETIC
MEMORABLE

Unlike all of the other positioning elements, the brand has two distinct functions that are separated in time. Upon its initial exposure to target consumers, it is important that its first function is to add character to the selling proposition. This is character that will stimulate consumer interest on initial contact, causing them to engage in the selling proposition. Google is such an example. It's cute and colorful and even fun to say. During this initial period there are three additional secondary characteristics that are important as well. These are "short", "poetic" and "memorable".

Short is a virtue for a reason you may not suspect. If a brand name is short, it will accommodate being made prominent at the impact point. That may be a website homepage, a brochure, a retail shelf, an ad, etc. Often it will be

so prominent that it becomes an attention-getting graphic device. One place to observe this phenomenon is to open your Internet browser. No matter what you are doing, you will more than likely encounter that cute and colorful Google logo within the first 30 seconds.

Another place to observe this phenomenon is in the laundry detergent category of your local supermarket. *Tide* set the standard for a bold brand typeface and all that have followed have created short names and hired package design experts to make them as bold as possible.

"Poetic" is important and needs to be distinguished. For our purposes lets assume that poetic refers to how smooth and rhythmic the brand name sounds. This effects how easily it is said in conversation. This poetic feature makes it easy for target consumers to integrate it into their psyche. Beyond their general awareness, it also facilitates easy recognition of what it now stands for. What it now stands for is what you communicate in your selling proposition. *Google* is an extraordinary example of a poetic word that otherwise had absolutely no point of origin or reference. Once you hear it, you are forced to remember it without the advantage of prior association, yet it is so poetic, it is hard to forget.

"Memorable" is strongly related to poetics in that, typically, highly poetic words are also memorable. Memorable is an obvious virtue to have in a brand name and worth vigorously pursuing. The *iPod* is an extraordinary example of memorable. In fact, the *iPod* includes all four characteristics required for the prefect brand name. It is short, poetically easy to see and say, and thus memorable. In addition, it has character if you simply consider its literal meaning: "information pod". All this combines to make a great tool for advertising and promotion.

Memorable can also be achieved by transplanting a well-known name from one category to another when it has some semblance of application in its new environment. I was recently reminded of that while driving down La Cienega Boulevard in Los Angeles. I noticed a business with an absolutely remarkable brand name. That name, applied to the building in a remarkable way was "The Merchant of Tennis". It's now five years later, and though still unique and cute, it's by definition no longer remarkable.

Your brand name then is simply a tool to make it easy for the target consumer to identify and reference your product. They will accept it no matter what. We have never heard of a name being rejected by consumers. They will drag it to the left side of the paradigm almost instantly and that is what you want. The additional positioning elements do the important positioning work; they are the elements that continue to evolve over time. It's their job to keep your product remarkable; the brand's purpose is to simply facilitate recognition.

After fairly short exposure to target consumers, the function of the brand will go through a fundamental change in terms of how consumers use it. That time can be as short as only one or two buying cycles. The more frequent the buying cycle, the faster it will happen. At this pivotal point, your target will have experienced your product or service, and whatever your brand name once meant to you, it will now mean whatever your target consumers' experience of it was. In other words, from that moment on, the importance of your brand name will be represented as you see here, with "characterizing" now at the bottom:

SHORT
POETIC
MEMORABLE
CHARACTERIZING

Again—at this point your brand, no matter what you named it, has become the sum total of your target consumers' experience of it. That is worth repeating: Your brand is the sum total of your target consumers' experience of it. Nothing else. Has the *Apple* computer brand ever caused you to think about the produce section of the supermarket? No. You immediately think of whatever your experience of it has been. Stop for a moment and think of a brand that you don't like. Now recall one that you do like. Note that your impression is solely based upon your experience of it and not your interpretation of its name or its image. This is no different than in life. As with a brand, who you are is the sum total of the experiences that others have of you. If your name is Daisy, are you a flower? Daisy is whatever her reputation is and so it goes, too, for your product or service. In this respect, your product or service name is irrelevant as long as the target consumer can easily remember and reference it.

The impact of "who you are" and how to control the target consumers' perception of it became an issue a couple of years ago for *Kentucky Fried Chicken*. Have you ever considered the motivation behind its name change to *KFC*?

I was not there when the decision was made, but I certainly agree with it. From the 1980s forward, we have seen a move toward foods that are "good for you". Notice I did not say "healthy". In reality, healthy has never been very big and will likely never be. Let's face it—we know certain foods are killing us, but we eat them anyway. "Tastes good and is good for you" has been a much stronger selling proposition than "healthy".

In the late 1980s, the government began publicizing studies that condemned the high-fat diets associated with fast foods. The word "fried" had been considered unhealthy for a long time, but after that it became so negative that marketers in general dropped it when characterizing their products. You can imagine the problem of dropping it when it's literally part of your name.

Based on my experience, I think I can safely speculate that the change from *Kentucky Fried Chicken* to *KFC* was a move to distance the brand from that bad "f-word", "fried". Chances are that Yum Brands (the brand owners) had research indicating that the name was holding them back. I am just as sure that subsequent research would indicate that, after the change, there's less of a "fried" consumer perception of the brand.

If you check out products in a supermarket, storefronts in a retail district, homepages on the Internet or leaf through the *Yellow Pages* of your phone book, you may be surprised to discover how many brands are simply the family names of their founders. It is difficult to find a brand of any significance that is still owned by its ancestors, yet many of their names remain. Nevertheless, over time, there has been a tendency to remove whatever family character was originally present. *Heinz*, *Hunt's* and *Del Monte* are three brands that have a rich family heritage that could easily bring more character to their selling propositions. However, the only thing that remains of their legacy is the ketchup. The same can be said for *Hertz* and *Avis*. Think about that in relation to the value of character. The value of character has never been more evident than with the Paul Newman brand. When it comes to buying food, there is no reason to think that Paul Newman's food is any better than other brands that have dedicated themselves to developing the best foods possible. Consumers purchase the Paul Newman brand to associate with its character, and its character has nothing to do with its food products. *Newman's Own* line of foods are based upon the late actor as a celebrity and the company's willingness to donate its profits to charity. That has nothing to do with food.

In the '90s, brand names experienced an identity crisis of major proportion. The Internet boom happened and the belief was that generic names were worth millions. Within the first two years it became clear that the name would get you started, but if that was the end of your business skills, you were in big trouble. Remember etoys.com? They went bankrupt. It took until now for a big company with a plan—*KB Toys*—to revive the once-dead website. Same thing happened to jewelry.com, only now brought back to life by Patrick Byrne, CEO of *Overstock.com*. Today the Internet is in full swing as it begins to fulfill its potential. Notice how few successful Internet businesses have generic names as opposed to poetic names with character such as *Google, Amazon, Skype, Yahoo!* and so on. These businesses do not exist because of their names, but because of their selling propositions—selling propositions perceived as remarkable by their target consumers.

The Internet now represents extraordinary opportunity for anyone with the creativity to invent a relevant business and the ingenuity to communicate it with a remarkable selling proposition. In some respects it is "virgin" territory in that it is driven by two kinds of people, neither with any marketing expertise. Most sites are constructed by website designers who are technically driven. They are well schooled in constructing a site and making it work but are short on marketing knowledge. In addition, many sites are given a look by graphic designers well schooled in that field but are also short on marketing knowledge. If you are like me, you have probably noticed while surfing that few sites make it easy to understand what the product is, what its benefit is or why I should buy it. If you are launching a business on the Internet, you are definitely on the right track reading this book—you will be a pro among millions of amateurs.

Brand names are only part of the brand image. Graphic treatment and subject matter are also a great way to add character. In 1998, I observed a change in the Orville Redenbacher brand that defies logic. The brand has been based upon the character of an unusual man who started selling popping corn out of the back of his car in 1960. By 1971 he was selling *Orville Redenbacher's* Gourmet Popping Corn in most supermarkets in the country and had begun to appear in his own TV commercials. He sold his company to Hunt-Wesson (now ConAgra Foods) in 1976 and continued appearing in the TV ads for the next 16 years. In 1992 he turned his advertising duties over to his look-alike nephew Gary. Mr. Redenbacher died at age 88 in 1995.

Only a couple of years after his death, the brand team concluded that Mr. Redenbacher's image on the front of the package had become inappropriate; they considered it outdated. Instead of updating it to make it relevant for the time, they removed it completely. This occurred at a time when aware marketers were working to add character to their product or service images given what we had discovered about the value of character. Skip ahead to 2006, when a different brand team brought Orville back using the same outdated image that had been pulled off in 1997. I don't have access to the market share for that category over those nine years without Orville but I would bet a steak dinner that they lost at least 5% of their market share...and that's severe.

In the early '80s I got a call from the new owner of an established regional baking company located in Southern California. It, too, was previously family owned and branded with the family name, Van de Kamp. The *Van de Kamp's* packaging at that time had been designed to make it look like a modern company. Their packages were all dark blue with a heavy typeface and a brightly colored, heavily stylized windmill trademark in the style of Peter Max. It looked quite modern and not at all like a brand with a heritage. The family had sold it many years before, and the new owner was convinced that *Entenmann's*, an Eastern brand, would enter the Southern California market within the year, and he wanted to be prepared. His direction was for us to create a new image that would reflect *Van de Kamp's* great family heritage.

I recall thinking initially that the company was appropriately located in the original building that the family had built more than 80 years before. Over the next couple of weeks, I had occasion to revisit the marketing team, which gave me additional exposure to the building. It was a two-story structure with a three-story facing on it. Way up at the top, for the most part unnoticed, I spotted the faded original logotype. It had remained long after the neon tubing had weathered away.

You guessed it—I recreated it. Then I added a windmill and presented it to the president. He praised it as authentic looking and did not recognize that I had ripped it off the front of the building until a week later when I pointed it out. I wanted to see if he would notice on his own… he didn't.

The *Van de Kamp's* bakery as a business entity closed its doors in the mid '80s. However, you can still see the brand hard at work on the shelf at any Ralph's supermarket. Its character is as valid as it was when the *Van de Kamp's* family established it back in the early 1900s. Can you imagine how the family would feel knowing that the brand has become a cover-up for *Ralph's* private label? Not likely what its founders intended.

I recently drove by the old building, now abandoned and boarded up. I was happy to discover that the sign remains, long after the family and all those who owned it over the past 100 years are gone.

Once more when creating a new brand, most people anguish over trying to make it define the product. We have never seen a brand name that fully defines a product. If it characterizes the product, that's perfect, but there's no need to define it. Names like *Google, Splenda, Tide* and *Amazon* tell you nothing about the product or service that each provides and it is not at all necessary that they do. They are simply identifiers of a product or service.

The Sub-Brand

The sub-brand is a completely different animal. Unlike the brand, the sub-brand's primary function is not to be a product or service identifier, but the reverse. Its function is to add character and pull a group of products or services together under the larger brand. The sub-brand's goal is to bring remarkability through appropriate character; this is perfectly demonstrated by *Yoplait*'s sub-brand, *Go-Gurt*.

When *Yoplait* decided to sell yogurt to kids, it seemed impossible; kids were simply not going to eat *Yoplait* yogurt. But, put it in a tube and characterize it in a fun way and you have a huge opportunity. Notice the prominence and character of the word "*Go-Gurt*". Think of it on its first day in the supermarket and you will see its remarkability.

For years, marketers avoided sub-brands as they insisted that advertising support was needed to make them a household word. They rationalized that the only function of the brand name was recognition and they applied that same thinking to the sub-brand name. In truth, recognition has never been the function of a sub-brand; it need not ever be a household word (great if it is, but not a requirement). It is a device to heavily characterize one or a group of key products within the larger brand—i.e., a tool to distinguish these products by adding character.

Examples of sub-brands exist in all categories. The *Microsoft XBox*, the *Nintendo Wii, Google Gmail, Yoplait Go-Gurt, Trojan's Magnum* and the *Old Spice Red Zone* are but a few obvious references. There are two marketing circumstances that make creating a sub-brand to your advantage.

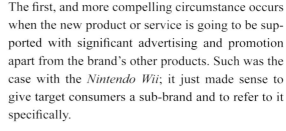

The first, and more compelling circumstance occurs when the new product or service is going to be supported with significant advertising and promotion apart from the brand's other products. Such was the case with the *Nintendo Wii*; it just made sense to give target consumers a sub-brand and to refer to it specifically.

A second circumstance occurs when a new product or service is created, and its point of difference is significant when compared to existing products in the line. In a case like *Microsoft XBOX 360*, you can see that it needs to be characterized, as it bears no relationship to its parent brand, which is known for its computer software.

These days there are many great examples of sub-brands to study. *Google* created *Gmail* and cleverly colored the characters in its logo as they appear in the parent brand yet had the insight to subordinate the brand logo in size and to pull the color out of its typeface. The *Google* brand acts as a credible endorsement for its *Gmail* sub-brand.

The *Old Spice* brand has been in the body fragrance business for more than 50 years, beginning as an after-shave lotion. Now in the deodorant business, their *Red Zone* sub-brand is used to communicate an ability to deal with strong body odor in heavy-duty athletic situations. The *Red Zone* refers to the last 20 yards on the football field before the end zone. Supposedly this area sees the toughest action during a game.

Trojan is another brand targeted to men. It too, has been around for more than 50 years, and it has been the leader to this day in marketing condoms. Their *Magnum* sub-brand characterizes their largest-sized product. The word "magnum" refers to the size of the inside of a gun barrel; it became a household word after the first Dirty Harry movie when Clint Eastwood carried a .44 Magnum revolver and used it with great

proficiency on the bad guys. I will leave the inference to you, but it would seem to be a sub-brand that any self-respecting male would aspire to. I wonder what percentage of *Magnum* condoms is purchased simply to enhance the image of the purchaser in the checkout line.

Segments

The next positioning element on the list is segments. They are used to break down a large number of products or services into groups that can be supported with separate advertising and promotion campaigns. Here's why.

Similar to the sub-brand, segments will typically characterize a small group of products or services that have something in common. If one segment is characterized with a sub-brand, the remaining segments should be sub-branded in kind. The opportunity for remarkability exists not only in the individual naming, but in the remarkability of the system itself.

The *3M SandBlaster* line was segmented into three work tasks at a time when all sandpaper was generically differentiated by grit. "Bare Surfaces", "Between Coats" and "Paint Stripping" are segments working together to bring remarkability to these products. Before *SandBlaster*, sandpaper was typically selected by target consumers using their thumbs to feel the grit and guess which one was right for their particular task. Segmentation by work task was perceived as a breakthrough by target consumers and they purchased the products in large quantities.

One of the goals of a consumer goods brand is to get as many products authorized as possible in order to capture as much shelf space as possible. That

not only increases sales but helps boost brand awareness. Segmentation can support that effort.

The trade will generally not authorize the full line of products for any given brand. You can check that out by going to the website of any of your favorite brands to discover the varieties of their products that did not make it into your local store. Their full line will likely be twice as large as the one you see displayed at your local retailer. A typical example would be a line of twelve products with six authorized for display. Going from six to twelve authorized products is simple; we increase the line to eighteen items and then divide them into two functional segments of nine each.

Let's say we launch a core line of nine frozen side dishes and entrees, and with our second line a reduced fat and calorie segment also with nine products. The trade then authorizes six from each segment and we now have twelve items on the shelf. We will never get to all eighteen until we buy the store, but without the segmentation we would have never gotten to twelve. That is exactly how *Stouffer's* did it; as a second segment, they added "*Lean Cuisine*." Don't hold me to the exact numbers, but you get the point.

There is an epilogue to the *Stouffer's* example. Subsequently they introduced a new segment that they have sub-branded, "*Corner Bistro*". It looks like an upscale line of dinners that's an alternative to their traditional *Stouffer's* line. It is priced higher and you can bet they would love consumers to trade up to generate additional profits. I counted three different products in my super-market then checked their website to discover they have six in the line. If

"*Corner Bistro*" is a hit, you can count on it becoming their third segment.

While I have given you many examples of sub-brands, only a very small percentage of brands actually have sub-brands.

The Benefit

In our work we have noticed that clients have an overwhelming fascination with their brand or sub-brand name. For the most part they think that success or failure is largely driven by it. Nothing could be further from the truth. The most important communication element of your selling proposition is absolutely not your brand or sub-brand; in reality, its a combination of two elements that morph into one. The first of those elements is the benefit. Its importance lies in its relevance to your target consumer. The benefit is best defined as what your target consumer gets out of experiencing your product or service. It's not about your product of service—it's about them, your target consumers.

For years, marketers have been adding "bullet points" to the selling propositions of their products and services. Bullet points are simply those short one or two-word claims that you see as you encounter various selling propositions. Some times you will see one by itself but it is more common to see two or three listed together. There is a time in the launch phase of a product or service when the marketing people call a meeting, sit down and debate exactly what bullet points should be emphasized. They think of and refer to all of these claims as "benefits" when in fact they rarely are. For the most part they are product attributes.

Attributes are simply characteristics of the product. During this time the marketers are so into the significance of their product or service that they lose track of addressing what their target consumer gets out of using it. That is a benefit. They seem only to be able to think about the features of their product or service. Very selfish thinking.

After much consideration of all that they have learned up to that point, decisions are made…bullet points are selected. The final cut is always organized in the same manner. A short list. "Made with 100% BLANK," or "contains all-natural BLANK," or "won't BLANK," and so on. In many instances, they don't relate to each other. They are simply arranged in the order of perceived importance. After years of exposure to overstated or over-promised bullet points, target consumers have developed the habit of simply ignoring them or at a minimum, discounting them.

Even when the bullet points are delivered using bold graphics, consumers ignore them en masse. As far as the consumer is concerned, bullet points are absolutely unremarkable; they've seen them all. They simply roll their eyes and move on to the next selling proposition.

This process usually causes the selling proposition to be organized in bits and pieces. That is a big problem given the mind works in generalities. The mind prefers complete thoughts. Do not expect the target consumer to pick up the bits and pieces and assemble them into your selling proposition. They will simply tune out and dismiss your product as unremarkable and unworthy of consideration.

The key to understanding this phenomenon is not so much in the information contained in all these bullet points, as it is in the overall context in which they are perceived by the target consumer. You see, a list of attributes is all about your product or service. A list of attributes has no consideration for what the target consumer gets. Over time we have made several key observations relative to the function of the benefit. As a result, we developed a method for you to communicate your benefit in a way that is perceived as remarkable by target consumers, that I will share here.

A benefit is typically what marketers refer to as a "why-to-buy". A why-to-buy is simply a claim that answers the question, "Why should I buy this product or service?" It addresses what the consumer gets out of using the product or service. It can also be in the form of a "call to action". I will demonstrate both.

Let's assume you are marketing *Benadryl* allergy relief medicine. Here are two possible benefits, one, a why-to-buy and the other, a call-to-action. The why-to-buy: "Relieves Symptoms Now." That is straight to the point and appears rather powerful on the surface. Looking closer you may observe that it is a general statement relative to the product. Still, it seems perfectly appropriate as is.

Now consider a one-word change that will give the statement a whole new meaning. I am referring to a call-to-action that reads "Relieve Your Symptoms Now." Notice two distinct characteristics that were missing before. First, this statement is not about the product as it was before, it's now about the consumer. Second, it suggests that the target consumer needs to do something now in order to benefit from using the product. As long as the target consumer considers the statement appropriate, the more personal call-to-action will always score well above the why-to-buy in research.

Now is your opportunity to take a look on page 213 at how you phrased your benefit. If it's in the form of a why-to-buy, take some time to see if you can restate it as a call-to-action. If you are successful in doing so, you may well move this positioning element from the left side of the paradigm to the right where all things are perceived as remarkable.

A great example of a why-to-buy benefit is seen in the following demonstrated under the brand name Central Pharmacy. Apparently, its owners wisely realized that the first part of their brand name, "Central", was relatively unimportant and so they subordinated it (look close) to their generic descriptor "Pharmacy". After all, people look for pharmacies, but without a lot of advertising support, they will not be looking for "Central". Given this scenario, they wisely dropped their benefit, "The Healthy Body Shop", right underneath the generic descriptor where it will experience high visibility. Very unusual and smart positioning; who wouldn't want a healthy body? Apparently, the Central Pharmacy is where you shop to get one.

Also rich in benefit copy is the ad for the Millennium anti-aging clinics. The headline, "Reclaim Your Youth", is a benefit likely to appeal to anyone over age 30. Under the heading "Our patients report" is a list of four specific benefits that are even more personal.

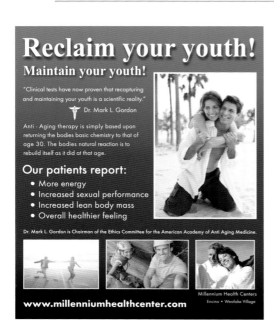

Now here's a bold statement related to the benefit. Ultimately, all products and services have the same optimum benefit. Yes, all. Being aware of this is your access to understanding the nature of the most powerful benefit you can create for your product or service.

In one of my seminars, I conducted the following exercise. It began as I solicited a volunteer from the audience willing to share a little about his product. While Mike did the exercise aloud, I asked that the other participants do it as well for their respective businesses.

KEITH: What is your product?

MIKE: Suntan lotion.

KEITH: Okay, Mike, what are the key attributes of your product?

MIKE: Our lotion allows an even tan while blocking UVA and most UVB rays.

KEITH: Okay. Given that, what is the product benefit? Or put another way, what does your target consumer get out of using your product?

MIKE: They get an even tan and a safe tan.

KEITH: Which of those two benefits, even or safe, do you consider the strongest?

MIKE: Both together.

KEITH: Okay, Mike, I can work with two. Now tell me what is the benefit of your target consumers getting both an even and safe tan from using your product?

MIKE: They look great.

KEITH: Now what is the benefit of that?

MIKE: They will be more popular.

KEITH: Okay, and what is the benefit of being popular?

MIKE: People will like them.

KEITH: And the benefit of that?

MIKE: A great life.

KEITH: Great, Mike, and what is the benefit of having a great life?

MIKE: It makes you happy.

KEITH: Very good! Then your suntan lotion has the same ultimate benefit as cat litter— or any other product. It makes you happy.

I have conducted this exercise many times with countless different products and services and the outcome is always the same. Target consumers, no matter what the category, ultimately want to be happy. They want your product or service to give them access to that happiness. I find that incredible and not a coincidence, as well as information that can be of extraordinary value if you understand its significance and put it into action for yourself and your product or service.

Look closely at the ultimate universal benefit chart for cat litter and allergy medicine. I have picked these two intentionally for their contrast. Note the ladder-like hierarchy as you scan from the bottom up. Also, notice that there is more about the product at the bottom of the ladder and more about the target consumer at the top.

Remember that all benefits define what the target consumer gets out of using the product or service and, by definition, are not product or service specific. The benefit is not about the product or service but about the target consumer.

The lesson here is that the higher you climb up the ladder, the more personal the benefit becomes. The more personal the benefit, the more it will relate to your target consumer, and therefore, it will be significantly more powerful. At the same time, you must be careful not to violate the truing principle we cov-

ULTIMATE UNIVERSAL BENEFIT

Cat Litter	Allergy Medicine
Happy	Happy
Great Life	Great Life
Odor-Free Home	Allergy-Free
Odor-Free Litter Area	Non-Drowsy Relief
Odor-Free Litter Box	Symptom Relief

ered earlier; it must be appropriate. Note that in this conversation, we only barely distinguish between a human and a product. When you get personal, the line between patronizing and authenticity becomes extremely fine. Target consumers will always interpret appearing authentic as appropriate, but if there is even a slight hint of being patronized, they will reject your selling proposition as inauthentic. Better safe than sorry on this one. If you think you're getting too personal, research it—the penalty for going over the line is target consumer mass rejection.

Looking a Little Further

What I am sharing with you here is based on a series of reliable observations. On the second ultimate universal benefit chart that follows, I have added (in red) the effect that the product has on the target consumer. If you look at the bottom row, the benefit is at a level of personal involvement with the product; the target consumer has something that makes the benefit possible—in this case, an odor-free litter box.

ULTIMATE UNIVERSAL BENEFIT

		Cat Litter	Allergy Medicine
Being	►	Happy	Happy
Having	►	Great Life	Great Life
Having	►	Odor-Free Home	Allergy-Free
Having	►	Odor-Free Litter Area	Non-Drowsy Relief
Having	►	Odor-Free Litter Box	Symptom Relief

Conversely, at the top, where the target consumer is simply happy, it does not seem to include awareness of the product. On the surface, this may look as if the product has gotten lost, but not so; the product is included within the ultimate benefit. It's just that the target consumer is no longer burdened with awareness of it—the relationship with the product is so complete that no other product would ever be considered, even if the target consumer were made aware of a strong alternative selling proposition. At this level, they will not go elsewhere.

This level of consumer commitment is indeed difficult to achieve, but it can be done. To maintain it, a consistent and ongoing effort to evolve the target consumer's perception of the product or service—through the appropriate and continuing application of character—is essential.

You now know how to identify a powerful benefit, which is a good thing. Let's assume for the moment that you have, in fact, identified a great benefit, the best that is humanly possible for your product or service. It is still most likely considered unremarkable by your target consumer. You may think your benefit is perfect and you may love that you can legitimately claim it, but your target consumer still considers it "BS". They've seen it before—maybe in another category—but it doesn't matter; it is simply unremarkable. Not fair but nonetheless true. On a remarkability scale of 1 to 10, you have a 3 because it's just one more bullet point to them.

An extraordinary example of a benefit that is extremely personal is in the selling proposition on the *Ensure* package that follows. In this case, the benefit "Healthy Mom" is apparently considered so important that it has been elevated to the role of the sub-brand. The *Ensure* brand has grown aggressively over the past 10 years. At one time it was simply a drink that offered a dense dose of nutrients and was primarily targeted to older people with poor eating habits. The medical profession was also targeted and many doctors routinely recommended it.

Looking closely, you will notice the "Healthy Mom" benefit statement is not at all about the product; it's appropriately about the target consumer. An even closer look reveals a clever characterization of the happy mom to reinforce the statement as well as to establish that the target is not an elderly person. It doesn't get much better than this. Or does it?

Consider the possibility that while the expectant mother considers her health extremely important, she may believe her baby's health or happiness even more so. Here's a possible ladder of benefits for this product, from the bottom up:

BENEFIT LADDER

1) Happy Baby
2) Healthy Baby
3) Happy Mom
4) Healthy Mom

If in fact the first three are subordinate to 1) Happy Baby, then there is an opportunity here to create a benefit line even more personal and more powerful than "Healthy Mom." My personal experience in this category is that this is very likely the case.

Of course, we must always be mindful to be perceived as appropriate. If we used a reference to the baby that was inappropriate, the selling proposition would be flatly rejected. In any case, the *Ensure* team's elevation of

this benefit statement to a sub-brand is brilliant marketing that I can only assume must be working.

The most frequent, and flagrant, use of benefits is seen at your local magazine stand. Find any vanity publication and you will be bombarded with benefits beyond your wildest dreams.

If you care to count, there are eight on the cover of this *Fitness Rx* magazine. In the magazine publishing business, these benefits are called "blurbs". These and the overstated bullet points are the reason that consumers discount the sincerity of all unsupported benefit claims.

Empowering Your Benefit

Good news—you can empower your benefit even though it is unremarkable. You can give it the credibility and strength it deserves, but not by adding the *Good Housekeeping* Seal or the endorsement of the AMA, CIA or any other organization. That's not the way it's done.

Over time we discovered a special relationship between two of the positioning elements. This relationship is truly significant because virtually no one is aware of it…that includes your competition. I recently took a methodical walk through a supermarket and a drug store, and only saw it on three products. They were all packages created by me, so I can safely say at this point that no one else is aware of this phenomenon. Given the current state of the marketplace, even if you execute it less than perfectly, you will be well ahead of your competition. I do, however, expect that it will become common practice now that it has been exposed here. That's the way it goes when something works.

This insight is based upon the relationship between the product benefit and its attributes. The opportunity that this insight represents was revealed in the series of observations that I just shared. Up to now, consumers consider benefit claims unremarkable as well as unbelievable. We are going to change that.

This 100%-effective method is based upon empowering your benefit in such a way as to have it perceived as remarkable by your target consumer. It is done by adding "attribute drivers" to the benefit that validate and empower it.

But first, turn to page 213 and review your earlier answer to question four. Now that you fully understand the nature of a great benefit, you will likely be able to improve your response.

Attributes

Attribute drivers are physical characteristics or performance features of your product or service that validate the claim you make when you state your benefit. They must directly relate to the benefit in order to qualify as drivers.

Many marketers also refer to them as "reasons to believe". You will remember that your benefit is a short statement of what your target consumer gets out of using your product or service. That statement is basically unbelievable by itself. Attaching the correct attribute serves as a reason to believe the claim you have stated in your benefit.

The age-old practice of prioritizing three or four of the most important selling features into bullet points and lining them up is a trap. Consumers interpret even the format as unremarkable and will dismiss most of the communication. Do not construe this as an absolute; it is a relative relationship, but a dramatic one. If you list the bullet points in the old-school way you may still be successful, but if you change the message as I suggest here, it becomes far more powerful. The differences may appear subtle until you look closely; I can promise the discrepancy in the consumers' reaction is significant. Intent-to-buy scores go much higher in research, and target consumers purchase more stuff. How much more convincing do you need?

There are basically three kinds of attributes: physical, performance and negative. Physical attributes are tangible characteristics of the product or service. Water is wet, clear and fluid. Performance attributes are what the product does when it is being used. Sugar sweetens, enhances flavor, increases calories. Negative attributes are those that address a possible negative product characteristic that needs to be overcome. Fruit juice has no artificial flavors or preservatives.

Typically you will see attributes used to communicate those features of a product or service that the owner feels will stimulate the target consumer to buy. Attributes, however, can be used in a much more powerful way.

Ordinary attributes become what we refer to as "drivers" when they are used to support the claim you make when you state your benefit. Another way of looking at them is that they empower your benefit. In order to do so, they must directly relate to the benefit and be located directly following the benefit. Attributes, when following and driving benefits, function together forming that reason for target consumers to believe I referred to.

It is important to understand that exploiting this relationship goes beyond simply communicating both benefit and attribute. The general proximity is what makes it all work as a unit. The proximity of this relationship is demonstrated below. Your benefit is a short statement of what your target consumer will get out of using your product. It is typically simple and, by itself, can range from unremarkable to significant. It is also larger than its drivers to reinforce their relationship, the benefit being dominant and the attribute drivers being supportive. Irrespective of its effectiveness, you will influence its impact greatly by adding attributes that "drive" it to remarkability when located directly adjacent to the benefit...preferably following it:

> **BENEFIT**
> • Attribute
> • Attribute

You will likely have a number of product attributes that you consider powerful. Some will relate directly to your benefit and some will not. Do not combine those attributes that do not support your benefit directly with it. My experience is that if you do, your target consumer will mentally disconnect from your selling proposition. Even if you consider the attribute extremely important, it must relate directly to your benefit or the two will appear out of sync. Location is everything. Let me demonstrate.

Let's say you are selling sandpaper and your benefit is simply, "Less Work".

You want to communicate that if your target consumer uses your sandpaper, they will do less work. Now here's the truth. If I handed you a sheet of sandpaper and said, "Here, use this—it's less work", you would roll your eyes in disbelief. By itself it is overused and simply isn't powerful.

Let's also say that your sandpaper has three attributes that you think are remarkable: 1) "Cuts 3 Times Faster", a powerful performance attribute; 2) "Clog Resistant", a powerful physical attribute; and 3) "Lasts 3 Times Longer", also a powerful performance attribute. The first two relate directly to "Less Work" and "drive" it. In fact, they push it to the remarkable side of the paradigm as observed on the accompanying *SandBlaster* package.

Now that "Less Work" has been empowered, you can see that target consumers will get the complete communication at a glance. The target consumer need not do much thinking to draw the desired conclusion. They are not required to assemble your communication to draw a conclusion to buy. Combining these three elements creates a powerful remarkable trigger that was not otherwise possible.

The third attribute, however—"Lasts 3 Times Longer"—does not relate directly to less work. To maximize its effectiveness it should not be placed close to it as if to support it. If you feel strongly that "Lasts 3 Times Longer" is important, find a location or another way of using it that is away from the "Less Work" benefit. Having said that, the *SandBlaster* positioning is very well done.

At this point, you can see the power of taking advantage of this benefit/attribute relationship and accept its logic. After having observed the effectiveness of arranging these two elements as I have suggested, I realized I really did not know why consumers responded so positively when we used it. Professional marketers always want to know why. Given that I routinely hang out in that crowd, discovering why became a goal of mine. It took over two years before I figured it out. The answer was, of course, in the nature of target consumers and how they think when encountering a selling proposition. More specifically, it is in the nature of how they encounter and deal with life itself.

Over time I have observed that humans are flooded with an endless stream of newly occurring stimulus in their lives. The nature of the stimulus they encounter is unanticipated and frequently negative. As a result, they have developed a defensive method for dealing with this phenomenon, one they are fundamentally unaware of. This condition is simply a permanent way of being.

Consumers appear to have developed a defensive filter that acts as an operating state. This mind set is "What's wrong here?" as I discussed briefly in chapter seven. Most selling propositions are unfortunately formed around product attributes that feed the target consumers' state of mind. When the initial message is about the product (attributes) and not about the target consumer, it is easy and natural for them to disqualify the product and move on, given that they are looking for "What's wrong here?".

A benefit occurs differently for consumers as it characterizes them, not the product. Doing so appears to eliminate the initial consumer objection caused by their operating state. At worst, they question the benefit, which is why we follow the benefit immediately with attribute drivers that support it. As marketers, understanding this process and working with it will give you a significant advantage over your competition. Bottom line: lead with your benefit and follow it with attribute drivers that empower it.

Here's a big fat attribute tip, I recommend that you incorporate metrics into your attribute drivers as often as you can. Target consumers appear to relate favorably to numbers. We think there is a natural presumption of significance when they are present. Additionally, there seems to be an assumption that you would not have used the numbers if they were insignificant. Look back one more time at the *SandBlaster* attribute drivers: "Cuts 3 Times Faster, Lasts 3 Times Longer". My personal experience is that the numbers were instrumental in its success. They were ultimately copied by the competition, further evidence of their effectiveness. What may seem insignificant to you may prove to be a driver to your target. I have seen "100% Natural" out-score "All Natural" many times but never the reverse.

Rarely, but now and then, there is an exception to always having the benefit supported by attribute drivers. It is rare that we would ever recommend it, but here is an extraordinary example of it. It occurs when the attribute is so compelling that it is believed to constitute a stronger trigger than its accompanying benefit.

In the photos on page 121, Cowan Natural Cleaners is all about its key product attribute, "Non-Toxic". "Non-Toxic" in this case is a physical attribute and an unusually powerful one. Apparently Mr. Cowan considered it more important than his own name. Take an even closer look and you'll see that Mr. Cowan went as far as to convey several benefits derived from his key attribute. He lists three that are all subordinate to the key attribute on his door:

> – "It's good for you"
> – "It's good for your clothes"
> – "It's good for your planet"

Good for you, Mr. Cowan. You recognized the power of this important attribute and you used benefits to drive it.

In the early '70s, *Hunt-Wesson* was eager to expand their *Hunt's* tomato brand into the spaghetti sauce category and also jumped on an attribute. At that time, *Ragu* dominated that business. The *Ragu* brand team was far more aggressive than most as demonstrated by their constant innovations. Even knowing that, the *Hunt-Wesson* team underestimated the tenacity of the *Ragu* team.

We were hired to do the package design. The brand team was responsible for its positioning. In their effort to enter the category, the *Hunt's* brand team had discovered a niche that *Ragu* had apparently missed. The team tested the physical attribute line, "Extra thick and zesty", which scored very well in several rounds of research. It had scored so well, in fact, that the *Hunt's* team decided to create three flavor variations in two sizes and launch them under a new brand. The new brand name was "Prima Salsa". This was before the proliferation of Mexican food in the late '70s, when Mexican salsas were introduced.

Unfortunately, the *Hunt's* team was not able to copyright the line "Extra thick and zesty". They proceeded in a way that would ultimately cause their downfall. Remember, we established earlier that the safest thing to do in this scenario is to elevate the remarkable trigger to a key feature. The *Hunt's* team's thinking was just the opposite. They led with their new brand Prima Salsa and dropped the "Extra thick and zesty" line into a small banner underneath it.

Hunt's launched its product and supported it with heavy advertising based on their attribute line "Extra thick and zesty." It was quite successful in the early months, taking a significant share of the category away from *Ragu*. That, however, came to a screeching halt in the seventh month when *Ragu* introduced its response. Their package featured a very small *Ragu* logo in the upper left corner of the package followed by a large, four-word sub-brand headline: "EXTRA THICK AND ZESTY." It was by far the most prominent feature on the package. Prima Salsa, whose advertising featured the line "extra thick and zesty," was now promoting the *Ragu* product every time they advertised. When consumers looked for "Extra thick and zesty." on the shelf, they saw the *Ragu* package and not the Prima Salsa package. Prima Salsa's life span was approximately 18 months.

To sum it up, Prima Salsa was never the trigger. The power was always in the attribute line "Extra thick and zesty." I would love to have known the *Ragu* team; in my mind, they had brains, awareness and guts in just the right proportions. Unfortunately, I was on the losing team that time but I never forgot the lesson. When I run into an element that is so remarkable that I believe it can be elevated in prominence, I do so in an attempt to own it.

A similar phenomenon exists when you run into a trigger created by the target consumer. This happens far more often than you might imagine. In the early '80s, we were working on the *Sparkletts* bottled water line. It is a brand owned by Danone (spelled correctly) Waters of North America which also owned *Evian, Dannon* and *Volvic* as well as others. At that time, the pull-top cap had been introduced by five different brands—*Sparkletts* was merely one of them. The pull-top was so popular that consumers began to refer to it as a "sport top". About nine months after its introduction, we designed the words "Sport Top" prominently into the *Sparkletts* label. In short time, the *Sparkletts* brand was given credit for this innovation and target consumers developed a loyalty to it. We simply assumed ownership of the trigger created by the target consumer, which lasted for more than 10 years.

You may have also noticed after being in business a little more than 30 years, Federal Express did exactly the same thing. You and I, as target consumers, changed its name. We so commonly referred to it as that the company had the foresight to change its name. Or, was the move ill advised? You can judge as

I share an abstraction.

The most sincere manifestation of adoration for a person or a product is to give him/her/it a nickname. It's a direct expression of affection, maybe even respect. But if you change your name to the nickname you've been given, you remove the possibility of other's expressing that adoration. I would have recommended Federal Express not make the change. I no longer have a cute, adoring way of characterizing *FedEx* and I miss that. It's been taken away from me, now that the company name is *FedEx*.

On the other hand, I have been banking with Washington Mutual, now Chase, for over five years and never have I heard it affectionately referred to as WaMu until they changed it and began advertising it. I find it awkward to pronounce, and if they had not heavily advertised it, I never would have figured out how they wanted us to pronounce it. In this case, I think they were trying to get us to warm up to them by creating their own nickname and forcing it on us. No matter now...it's Chase.

Negative Attributes

Negative attributes need to be distinguished because they are radically different from physical and performance attributes. Negative attributes typically do not drive business forward. They do, however, overcome key objections. If unanswered, you may not sell the first unit. The most common negative attributes are no artificial ingredients, no preservatives, no this or no that. The no, no, no—that's where the negative connotation comes from. You use them only when you must or when it is a requirement for being in a specific category because your competition is using it.

If you were about to launch a new aerosol spray, the likely objection would be that it might leave a residue. The "Leaves No Residue" line will save you a lot of resistance, but we do not think of it as driving business nor do we consider this a remarkable trigger.

If you look closely at the *Raid* Ant & Roach Killer package you will see the classic use of a negative attribute. This one is apparently a result of a consumer concern that products like these are associated with strong chemical odors. The *Raid* brand people apparently feel this one is ultra-important as it is contained inside of an attention-get-ting graphic "burst". It reads "No Lingering Chemical Odor" and is flanked by the words "New Formula", which function as a reason to believe.

Now that you are well schooled in the use of all three forms of attributes, let's return to page 213 and reconsider the attributes you listed earlier. If you identified any negative attributes that you consider important, they must pass a simple test to be used at your impact point. You must ask 10 of your target consumers the following question: "Will you buy this product if I do not put this on the label?" If three or more say "no", you must consider it significant enough to communicate at the impact point. If that occurs, you must not locate it next to your benefit; positioning it anywhere else where it will be perceived as a minor element of your selling proposi-tion is fine.

Next, I want you to consider identifying two attributes, either physical or performance, that you think might empower your benefit in such a way as to have it perceived as remarkable by your target consumer. Consider the nature of the two types we have identified. In my experience, performance attributes have been far more effective at accomplishing this than physical at-tributes. I am still looking for a good explanation for this phenomenon, so I can only offer what I consider to be a good guess.

I believe it is rooted in dynamic verses static mental imagery. I have observed in photography that, as an element of a selling proposition, the dynamic far out-scores the static. In other words, the action shot is much stronger than the still shot of the same subject matter. Action clearly stimulates more inter-est in a subject. This can easily be extrapolated to the mental imagery con-jured up by the target consumer when he or she is exposed to two different words within the same general context. Compare these two strong attributes of sandpaper: "Sharp Grit" or "Cuts 3 Times Faster". Can you see the static versus dynamic nature of these two attributes?

Now take 10 minutes and fine tune your product or service's key attributes on page 213. You are on your way to more remarkability. While you're there though, don't change your answer to question number six. You're on your way, but not there yet.

Relevant to You

At this point, there may still be a few of you telling yourselves that your product or service does not accommodate the distinctions I have just shared. No matter what you are selling, nothing could be further from reality. You have to look and explore. Complete selling propositions are presenting themselves to you constantly, but you must look. All of these distinctions apply, every single one. Some will be more important than others, but they are all relevant.

Here is an example you would not likely think of. One that is as far from the retail environment as possible, yet contains all of the distinctions I have addressed. I will venture that this product has been offered to all of us and we have decided to purchase it more than once. In fact, this product may represent one of the most successful selling propositions of all time.

You are driving along in your car and pull to a stop at an intersection. You notice a homeless man holding a piece of cardboard with some writing on it. You read the sign, reach into your pocket, pull out a dollar and give it to him. What you have just encountered is a complete selling proposition, one that is not just complete but also valid and apparently effective. This guy has no website, no retail package, no brochure, no billboard and no storefront, but he has an effective selling proposition, and he's communicating it. A close look will reveal that all the applicable communication elements to do the job are clearly present.

I guarantee that a benefit was present or you would definitely not have spent the money. Notice that I said spent the money. You spent the money and you can bet you got something for it. Think about it. Remember the most effective benefit is about the target consumer, not the product. Consider "peace of mind" or "ease of conscience". If you gave him the cash, something like that was present for you.

Given that, what attribute drivers were present? What physical or performance attributes were there to empower the benefit? Perhaps he was not wearing shoes? Was he unshaven? These are physical attributes (reasons to believe) that empower the benefit. Did he promise to wash your windshield or hand you a poem? These would be performance attributes that empower the benefit. Take another look at your product or service and perhaps you will see things more clearly.

Now that you are aware of the nature of great attributes, and of the benefit/ attribute relationship, turn to page 213 and review your earlier answer to question five. Feel free to change your attributes accordingly.

The Tag Line

Tag lines, next in the communications model, are easy to address given that they seem to fall into two distinct categories: big guys and the rest of us. The first category, the big guys, includes all of those tag lines that you can recall when challenged to do so at a cocktail party. Without question, the most prominent these days is "Just Do It." Tag lines like this are typically the invention of the advertising agency and are intended to go beyond the brand's name and image to add ongoing character for promotion purposes. Tag lines like these are literally not available to small, medium and most large businesses; they are reserved for huge businesses with the financial resources necessary to make them household words.

For the rest of us, the tag line can also be effective if conceived and used in a much different context, of which there are three. The first will be obvious if you can remember back to the generic descriptor section when we discussed adding character; we did so in order to have the generic descriptor perceived as remarkable by target consumers. The act of adding character literally turns the generic descriptor into a tag line, giving it meaning beyond simply defining the product. Here are two before and after examples are in order:

BEFORE	AFTER
Yogurt	Portable Yogurt
Marketing Secrets	Marketing Secrets the *Fortune* 100 use

Notice that these are effective at adding remarkability but have no chance of achieving the awareness of "Just Do It", nor is that the intended purpose. These are designed to work at the impact point.

The second context is simply a line created to address what we think is a compelling observation to the target consumer. Its message will relate to more than one communication element and is frequently used, to your best advantage, in the form of a "call to action".

Eckhart Tolle's book *A New Earth* has a prominent tag line on the front cover that is formed beautifully into a call to action. It reads, "Awakening to Your Life's Purpose". That is bold and cuts right to the heart of the universal question, "Why are we here"? He is challenging us to wake up and discover the purpose of life. If you are not offended by the "call to action", you will likely take the challenge and buy the book…I did.

The third is accomplished by developing a tag line that tends to make your

product or service important by attaching it to a cliché. The motion picture industry is famous for this technique. An example is the movie *The Reaping* with the tag line "What Hath God Wrought?", which is larger than the movie title. The marketing team most likely concluded that the tag line added more character than the title. It is also likely more memorable given it is a familiar line from the Bible.

Short is a key virtue of any tag line, and if you think three to five words is not enough to get it done, consider the following. An example of a two-word tag line comes from a brand dominant in the allergy relief category. *Claritin* has a great tag line that is short, poetic, memorable and a direct interpretation of the brand's benefit: "*Claritin* Clear". Not an over-promise, outrageous claim or a line that will wear out in six months. I particularly like this one because it is a benefit, and seems to be a powerful one. I say put this one on the package and locate a couple of attribute drivers nearby and consumers will respond.

In the early '70s, I was just getting started in the business and had a partner. He had secured the job of creating the key marketing brochure for a new cargo airline located at that time in Memphis, Tennessee. They were about to initiate business from Little Rock, Arkansas, with the breakthrough idea that they could fly small packages through the Little Rock hub every night and thereby offer America overnight delivery anywhere in the country. I had just gotten out of the Air Force and found the idea fascinating. My partner Rick, an avid civilian pilot, was also excited.

For the most part, Rick handled the account while I offered an opinion now and then. The tag line that got created also became the headline for the brochure and was used in the TV commercials that launched the business. It was a cliché—"Think Fast"—but, applied directly to the benefit, it worked beautifully. The key graphic on the cover of the marketing brochure was a photo of the aircraft at takeoff. It was shot at an angle to dramatically expose the new airline's name—that's right, Federal Express again. The "Think Fast" was located across the top of the cover.

I recall that the initial planes used by Federal Express were surplus Fanjet Falcon executive aircraft leased from Pan Am and temporarily converted to cargo aircraft. We only had one photo and had to clone it so it would look like we had a fleet. Rick did a great job and it paid off for the client.

If you develop a tag line you are enamored with—and that's easy to do—you want to be sure it adds to your selling proposition. A tag line may well push your selling proposition to the point of being more information than your target consumer is willing to deal with. Consumers are notorious for tuning out on a selling proposition that looks even mildly complicated at first glance.

The Endorsement

We have discovered that few endorsements are considered remarkable by target consumers. On the other hand, given their function of adding credibility, they can be quite useful if your brand is not familiar to your target consumers. An endorsement comes from an external authority of some kind. In order for it to work, it must be established in the mind of the target consumer, or at least appear credible to the target consumer. Given that they are familiar, they are unremarkable by definition.

The *Good Housekeeping* Seal has been used widely and seemingly forever. Our experience in working with it is that it is in a class by itself. It is not only considered unremarkable by target consumers, it also appears trite and of little value. In addition to its overexposure, we speculate its tarnished image is due to the fact that most any product can qualify to use the symbol if they purchase space in the magazine. Over time I suspect many consumers have experienced dissatisfaction with some of the products and services it has endorsed. If target consumers actually understood what little is required to display the seal, it would surely lose whatever little charm it has left. In our work, it seems to be of little value at this time. Endorsements are most effective in the area of over-the-counter medications and nutritional supplements; these products, purchased for the most part on a leap of faith, need the additional support.

I suspect that consumers in these categories are looking for reassurance rather than the instant gratification that they have become accustomed to in most other categories. You see, if you spent $25 on a quart of *Sauza* Tequila Hornitos 100% Puro de Agave, you will feel instantly gratified the second you do your first shooter. In fact, I can verify that the more shooters you do, the more gratified you'll feel (at least until the next morning). We consumers have come to rely on that instant gratification to validate our purchases.

If you had more money to spend and were interested in lowering your cholesterol and rehabilitating your joints, you might use it on two of *Nature Made's* nutritional supplements. If so, you'd experience an absence of short-term gratification, and would be looking for a reason to believe. The endorsement of the *Arthritis Foundation* works for the joint supplement, as

of your target consumer. It sets your product or service aside from whatever is around it at your impact point. Remember, your impact point is a physical place where your selling proposition (sales message)—always an element within your graphic presentation—is presented to your target consumer.

Understanding impact is relatively simple; accomplishing it without being inappropriate is a bit more difficult. You must do it and do it well, however, or your selling proposition will not get considered and your sales will suffer. The impact you are striving for is to appear unique at first glance so that you are considered the alternative in your category. That is to say your product or service is, right off the bat, considered so interesting that your target consumer wants to know more. They want to engage your selling proposition. This is normally accomplished in graphic form, word form, via a structure in a visual environment or with an unusual sound or simple phrase in an audio environment.

Therefore, think of impact as the first of two relatively simple experiences you want your target consumer to have. First, you want "encounter impact" that causes them to want to engage in your selling proposition. Second, you want your selling proposition to be remarkable enough so they decide to purchase. You need both. While they are simple to understand, they are nevertheless elusive.

You can see by the following photo that the *Special K*-branded cereals have a great deal of impact. They clearly stand out as an alternative in the category. Even though target consumers have likely considered them unremarkable by our definition, they continue to compete for new business by virtue of their powerful impact. *Special K* is most likely reconsidered daily by consumers who purchase other brands; its impact causes the others to fade by comparison. Can you imagine how the brand managers of the competitive brands feel as they wrestle with it daily?

Impact is also critical for retail

businesses, few of which distinguish themselves. The signing restrictions imposed by city regulations or the architectural dictates of the managers of strip malls can be extremely inhibiting. In the following photo, notice the Odyssey Video store has taken full advantage of the control they seem to have over

the building they inhabit; impact is accomplished by the use of a bold color and graphics.

The Hard Rock Cafe has the advantage of a significant level of consumer awareness. That awareness was not always there, but the oversized guitar was there since the opening of the first restaurant. It is a mnemonic that initially worked to symbolize the restaurant's theme and now functions as an instant identifier for the now-famous chain.

The Product Configuration

Product configuration is considered a critical part of positioning. Once again, let's look at *SandBlaster* sandpaper. Each of these three very different sandpapers was developed to perform a specific job. They have been appropriately color-coded to enable target consumers to easily identify and differentiate them. They truly perform in a manner consistent with the three work tasks you see here: Between Coats, Paint Stripping and Bare Surfaces. Can you imag-

ine how difficult sorting them out would be if all three were brown as in the old days?

The Container Configuration

The configuration of your container is a huge asset when introducing a new product or service. I will clarify my use of the term "container". All products and services being sold are packaged, and the container they are packaged in, must be considered yet another opportunity to be perceived as remarkable. Containers are more or less an opportunity, based upon what you are selling—a product or a service. It's easy to see that all packaged goods are candidates, but what about services? Let's speculate for a moment.

If you are a dentist, you could be located in a building that looks like a tooth. If you are in the broadcast industry, your building could look like a TV or radio. If you are a plumber, you might turn your van into a…well, you figure it out. These ideas may seem extreme, but consider if you were an independent donut shop having to compete with *Dunkin' Donuts*, or a small restaurant specializing in great-tasting hamburgers and hot dogs. Your container, your building, could be remarkable as demonstrated in the adjoining photos. When you look at them, don't you get the feeling that Randy's Donuts are special… remarkable? Don't you believe that Carneys hot dogs and hamburgers are extraordinary… remarkable?

In 2003, the *Folgers* coffee brand got a big boost by changing its container. The in-store coffee category had been declining at about 5% per year for a long time. Oddly enough, the success of *Starbucks* and others had little effect on the supermarket coffee category, which was considered stale and uninteresting. I suspect the interest in *Starbucks* is indicative of the experience that is simply not available with one purchasing coffee in the supermarket.

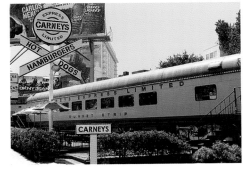

The break came when *Folgers* finally abandoned the old coffee tin in favor of a new plastic container. It was considered much "friendlier" to consumers who perceived that it would keep their coffee fresher. It also had a handle that made it much easier to grip and control than the old tin can. The result was strong positive consumer acceptance and a corresponding increase in the share of the category for *Folgers*.

In the mid '80s, I was asked to do a package design for a new line of juice drinks that featured football-shaped plastic bottles. They were cute, and basically a good idea. To accommodate the new bottles, a brand was developed with the endorsement of Marcus Allen, all-star running back for the Los Angeles Raiders. That seemed to be another good idea. The new bottle was approved, the package design was accepted and the client went into production. The concept was valid—a great product driven by a remarkable container and the remarkable endorsement of a popular athlete—but the product failed. It was unsuccessful due to a flaw in the bottle design. On the day the co-packer began filling the bottles, it was discovered that the bottle was too large. It held about 15% more product by volume than it was supposed to. The over-wrap cartons had already been printed, reflecting the lower-volume net weights.

At this point, the client had two choices and both were losers. They could slack-fill the bottles with the correct amount of juice knowing the consumer would notice and likely object. The second alternative was to fill each bottle to its capacity and absorb the cost. The client chose the second option, meaning he had to sell a lot of product to show a profit. He did it because he knew consumers were likely to complain about the slack-fill, which would cause the supermarket chains to return the product. That would have been a disaster, but at least a quick death. In retrospect it was the better option because he lost all his operating capital trying to reach the volume he needed to generate a profit. The business failed in less than a year.

I remember Donald Trump saying on *The Apprentice* that "The devil is in the details." He may have borrowed the line, but having adapted it to his business practice says a lot about Trump. Too bad he wasn't involved with this project.

Container configuration may also be important to a brochure. A new structure is likely to get the target consumers' interest well before they encounter the selling proposition. Someone recently left a door hanger at my house. It was long and hung down much further than any hanger I'd seen before. The graphic design of the accompanying brochure took full advantage of the hanger's unique shape, which made it even more remarkable. I couldn't wait to see what it was about. I was fully engaged and read it cover to cover, which I rarely do. That door hanger was the container configuration for its selling proposition, though, as it turned out, I was not the target for this particular product—wrong gender.

Container innovations are infrequent at best, but do come along. They are generally discouraged due to the almost certain added cost to the product. In the last few years, however, you may have noticed a consumer goods labeling innovation first introduced by the Fujifilm Company almost 10 years ago. In the past few years, it has become available at a cost considered affordable by most marketers who are jumping on board. It's a plastic film that's printed flat, then stretched over uneven surfaces making a very large graphic

area available when compared to a label. As a package designer, it's like a breath of fresh air to work with I can tell you. You see it here on the *Cheetos* and *Wishbone* packages. The "stretchy" flexible film allows typefaces to be 25% longer than they would be on a printed paper label. This, in turn, makes the whole package look 25% longer as the target consumer scans the shelf. That's a big advantage, and easily covers the first of those two essential functions of package presentation—grabbing the target's attention. I have noticed, as you may have also, that advertisers are now covering buses and buildings with graphics in a similar way. I wonder what's next?

In the mid '70s, the European Tetra Pak was introduced in the United States.

It is an extremely sterile container originally developed for areas of the world where refrigeration was limited. Believe it or not, that described all of Europe in the '60s and '70s.

The Tetra Pak is the rectangular box that you have been buying juice in for 20–plus years now. In the beverage category, it caught on fairly quickly with juice as moms and kids thought it novel to punch the little straw through the hole. Beyond juice, American consumers were slow to accept it in other categories.

In 1975, I was asked to work on a shelf-stable milk to be sold unrefrigerated in a Tetra Pak. As extreme as that sounds, even today, Canadians and Europeans were routinely purchasing warm milk, taking it home, storing it in their cupboards, then cooling it in their refrigerators before they served it. We worked diligently for a year and were not able to get Americans interested in it. Even now, in spite of its practical form relative to refrigerated milk, Americans are simply not interested.

For reasons unknown to me, environmentalists have laid off this container when, in reality, it is completely unfriendly to the U.S. environment. In most of Europe where environmentalists are quite influential, manufacturers are not permitted to glue materials together such as paperboard, plastic or foil, yet the Tetra Pak is the exception. Europeans have accepted and adopted it and have developed an industry to recycle it into building material. Here in the United States, it would require an enormous investment to follow suit. The Tetra Pak is a lamination of foil, plastic and paperboard, making its recycling impossible at this time in the States.

Now that I've indicted the Tetra Pak, it should also be noted that it is far superior to many of the containers we frequently use here in America, including the can. The Tetra Pak is absolutely sterile and has an extraordinary shelf life. You can open it without tools, cook or pasteurize in it, and you do not need preservatives. It also will not affect the taste of food in any way, no matter how long it sits. And when you pour out its contents, nothing sticks to the inside. Another big advantage is that it's cheaper than most of the alternatives, including the tin can.

In 2004, Hormel converted its *Stagg*-branded chili into the Tetra Pak to take advantage of the qualities I just described. In doing so, they became a pioneer in the chili category.

Irrespective of its advantages, it did not come to the chili category without problems. When first introduced, consumers had an issue opening it. You see, chili can't be sucked through a straw; consumers were familiar with the container, but not in this context. The procedure for opening the package was completely foreign. You and I, as consumers, have long-established behavioral patterns and this package did not fit any of them. Generally, teaching consumers new behavioral patterns is to be avoided at all costs, but not this time.

It wasn't until their chili had gone from the can to the Tetra Pak that the Hormel folks discovered the problem—and it was severe. Less than 10% of consumers could open it properly. It is in fact easy to open, but simply not part of our psyche. Although scissors were never intended as part of the process, most target consumers grabbed a pair to cut the top off and enjoy the chili.

Can you see that this is a positioning problem?
The container offers a benefit to the consumer but is not being communicated at all, let alone in a powerful way. We got the call and were assigned the task of finding the communication that would get across the appropriate opening procedure to the target consumer. Not as simple as it sounds.

It took well over 50 attempts before the problem was resolved. One of the critical steps is that the entire top of the package needs to be squeezed together. This turned out to be an act as foreign to consumers as breathing water.

You can see by the elaborate instructions on its front and top that opening it has become the single-most important positioning element of the selling proposition. Once we made the change, the advertising agency produced a commercial similarly targeted at the "squeeze" needed to open it properly, but that still wasn't enough.

Sadly, consumers did not fully embrace chili in the Tetra Pak. In 2007, the container was abandoned and *Stagg* Chili returned to the can. Sometimes it's just too tough to force new behavioral patterns on target consumers. For whatever reason, however, the *Campbell's* people seem to have had some recent success in selling soup and broth in the Tetra Pak.

The Product Presentation

Product presentation is not often remarkable. Frequently, the product is accurately presented in a straightforward manner conveying in the simplest terms exactly what it is. It shows up as remarkable when the product configuration itself is remarkable in appearance, like granola on top of yogurt. Beyond that, it is generally the responsibility of the remaining positioning elements to communicate remarkability. There are two categories in supermarkets that demonstrate the extremes in the quest for product presentation remarkability.

The first is frozen food. For some reason this category is stuck in what is characterized as extraordinary food photography that has appetite appeal as its goal. Next time you're strolling this section, take a look. Lots of good photography, and all the products look alike and always will. This is true in spite of the fact that manufacturers spend thousands of dollars on food stylists to make their offerings appear beautiful and unique. They're all beautiful, hence none are unique.

The second category, by stark contrast, is alive with innovation when it comes to product presentation. The category with all the action is breakfast cereal. Innovation in this category is so pervasive that target consumers expect it and have thus decreased the time in which it takes them to drag newly remarkable triggers back to the unremarkable side of the paradigm. As soon as it became known that many of the cereals with reasonably high fiber content were good for your heart, hearts began showing up throughout the category. That key graphic has become unremarkable simply because there are so many. I recently counted heart symbols on 16 different packages.

Notice the following two examples. *Kellogg's Raisin Bran* has developed a cute sun character adding scoops of raisins to a bowl of cereal. Then observe the *Apple Jacks* package where King Kong is seen swinging at flying pieces of cereal and milk. Both of these product presentations are innovative and were likely considered remarkable by target consumers when first introduced. Can you imagine how much more interesting and remarkable a little innovation like this would be over in frozen foods, down the street at your local gas station or even your bank or dry cleaner…why not?

Here's the proof that remarkability can be achieved through product presentation at your local dry cleaner. This one is right up there with the giant shoe car in that it instantly establishes the retailer's product.

Notice that the owner of Sterling Fine Cleaning decided to route his conveyer outside his building so all could see what he is up to; I also get the feeling he is proud of his work, or why would he display it so brazenly? Now I know you and I cannot see any difference between his cleaning and any other cleaners' work but the inference is clearly there. That conveyer is the same one you and I encounter in every dry cleaning establishment we have ever been in. It was absolutely unremarkable until it was rerouted to achieve remarkability. What's the lesson here? Look at your own business and reroute something to remarkability.

The Delivery System

Delivery systems can be strong remarkable triggers. If you are unclear exactly what a delivery system is, I will define it. The broad meaning is anything that enhances the process of accessing the product or service after the sale is made. With consumer products, it is often a feature of the container. I will site one of the oldest as well as one of the newest: *PEZ* and *Go-Gurt*. Others include buying stock or groceries over the internet. The delivery system can also be literal. My friend who owns the dry cleaning business offered pick-up and delivery service to his more affluent clients. It was remarkable when he launched it; now it's simply a significant part of his business. It's true—you really need to think of what happens after you make the sale; this is an element too often overlooked.

Think about it. When you were a kid, what would your reaction have been to a bowl full of *PEZ* candies? Would you have even recognized them, let alone eaten them? Or, what if they had been sold in a bag or a box? Consider that remarkability goes well beyond uniqueness; it's actually the "play value" that drives it. This is a distinction recognized, measured and calculated by the toy industry on a regular basis, but often overlooked in other categories.

Play value was a virtue first observed about 35 years ago when we noticed kids eating *Oreo* cookies. For some reason, many kids like to unscrew an *Oreo* before they eat it. In order for the dark part to be considered edible, the white creamy center must first be scraped off with their front teeth. The folks at *Nabisco* consider themselves blessed that their product has such incredible play value.

Go-Gurt comes in a plastic tube. Sure that makes it portable, but it also makes it a lot more fun to eat, and was key to having it be accepted by kids. Many of the marketers involved in the *Go-Gurt* project were convinced that its appeal was portability. As it turns out, that was never the case; it was always its play value.

After all, we were all kids at one time and that's when we developed our affinity for play value. I can assure you that play value remains alive and well in adults. Notwithstanding nicotine addiction, play value is exactly what cigarettes are all about. Surely you don't think cigarettes taste good or make your breath, hair and clothes smell nice? It's play value; a cigarette is something to fiddle with and was something to toy with long before it addicted its victims.

Quite recently, we presented a pipeline of new product concepts to a beverage client and the highest scoring of the bunch was the one we intentionally developed with play value. As a serious marketer, I am ever mindful of the fact that we all learned to play long before we discovered anything else. Think about it—that was all mom and dad could do with us in those early formative months. Remember when mom got you to open your mouth for the spoon loaded with spinach? She made it fun and you "ate" it up.

Earlier, I cited granola on top of yogurt as one of the elite 2% where a product is immediately perceived as remarkable upon sight because its delivery system is visible. In the early '80s, I was given another product to position that had the same virtue, a delivery system that was considered unique and remarkable upon first exposure to target consumers. This one was extremely clever, but also an example of a technology that the client was never able to make work.

It began with a lunch invitation from the new product manager of a regional water company. Over the meal, he exposed two new projects to me regarding products they had developed and that he wanted us to position to their target markets.

The first was easy. It was one of those Australian beverages that hit the U.S. about the same time that Paul Hogan, alias Crocodile Dundee, was selling Australian tourism through "shrimp on the barbie". We created a product called Wallaroo that took off like all the others at that time. But the second assignment was more to the point of a visible delivery system with technical problems.

This product was a *Sparkletts* branded line of four seltzers that came in heavy plastic bottles with plastic dispenser heads sold separately. The bottles were cool looking, as you can see, and the spritzer heads were sold on the Original Flavor bottle, also separately. We designed the labels to have that early authentic New York look and be fun as well. They were an instant hit and

SPARKLETTS BRINGS

EXCITEMENT!

management approved a national expansion within six months. That turned out to be premature as the technology was new and had bugs that needed working out. In this case, management was so wrapped up in their product's short-term success that they were over-eager to expand.

As it happened, this was one of those products that target consumers initially bought out of curiosity, which ultimately created inflated sales numbers. The rollout was in California where consumers are less critical and the ratio of "early adopters" is quite high. "Early adopters" is a marketing term referring to consumers who are eager to purchase anything they perceive as new and interesting; California is the home base and breeding ground for these folks.

In addition to inflated sales, other problems began to crop up. The bottles had to be under a great deal of pressure in order to work. Many leaked on the shelf, which irritated the stores. The pick-up and clean up got to be routine. The trade seemed satisfied with the promise that the problem had been identified and that the fix was imminent. I think they, too, were enamored of the unique bottle. Today the trade is much stricter and most likely would have told the *Sparkletts* people to pick it all up for good.

Some stores got confused and sold the bottles without stocking the heads, creating angry consumers. Without the head, it's impossible to access the product. If I recall correctly, that happened to the entire city of Phoenix. As bad as that was, there was worse. If by chance a consumer was successful at poking a hole in the plastic bottle, they would experience a noise equivalent to a shotgun blast.

One of the bottle suppliers failed to glue the plug in properly and they began blowing out in the Florida market. This was serious as the internal pressure was more than 2,000 pounds per square inch. There were several lawsuits that had to be settled, but that did not slow management who remained in love with their technology.

Finally, the national rollout was nearly complete. The last market was New York City, the home of seltzer and seltzer lovers. What could possibly go wrong there?

Unfortunately, the product was soundly rejected in New York. New Yorkers are not easily impressed, nor are they early adapters. While Californians saw play value in this novel product, the New York crowd saw it as a rip-off. They were used to buying a one-liter bottle of seltzer for 35 cents and did not see any virtue in spending $1.35 for a two-liter bottle just because it had a dispenser. Hell, they had only just gotten rid of the old bulky bottle they'd been using for years, and considered the miracle product to be that 35-cent plastic bottle that stayed fizzy without a problem. I don't know the extent of the losses generated by this product, but they were significant; this could have been greatly minimized by simply giving the initial test market time to settle down and then measure the product's true potential.

The lesson here is to not become so enamored with your own ideas that you lose touch with reality. This product charmed everyone but was ultimately never going to work because it was simply too expensive to produce. The fact that it was fraught with problems seemed to energize the marketing team and make them even more determined to force it into the market.

The Graphic Presentation

At your impact point, you will organize all of the communication elements critical to communicating your selling proposition into your graphic presentation. This is simply the layout encountered at your primary impact point as I have stated before. Graphic presentations come in the form of a homepage, retail package, storefront, billboard, etc. The most common example of graphic presentation at the impact point is on a consumer goods package. These packages force marketers to keep their message simple and to the point—you can judge and review thousands of examples of their skill in any retail store, supermarket, drugstore, etc.

We've observed that retail businesses (store fronts) are the best example of poor graphic communication at the impact point. For the most part, they settle for communicating their name and a generic descriptor defining what they sell. In fact, given what you know now, if you take the time to check the retail establishments in your area, you'll be surprised at how little they communicate about their selling propositions.

Your graphic presentation is 100% functional in that its purpose is to organize your selling proposition in a specific order. You will control exactly the order in which your positioning elements are revealed to your target consumer. I will demonstrate this through a series of real world examples. For now just presume that you have a consumer product and that all of the positioning elements apply in the order in which I am about to share them.

You must first identify your key impact point. All products and services have multiple impact points. For instance, if you were operating a dry cleaning company, your sales message is conveyed when target consumers encounter your store front, your *Yellow Pages* ad, your brochure and your website. Your key impact point is the one that you consider most important. Typically, that is the impact point that has the greatest number of exposures. Let's assume for the dry cleaning business it is the storefront.

As you proceed, you will need to choose your key impact point, which will be the subject of the work that you will do in developing a remarkable sales message. Once you have completed development of your remarkable sales message, as applied to your key impact point, you will reapply that information to your remaining impact points as appropriate. You also have the option to run additional impact points through the process one at a time.

As an example, our dry cleaning company might take the storefront through the process, then create their *Yellow Pages* ad and their brochure by using what they have learned.

The overall impact of your graphic presentation must set you apart from all others in your category. You must be considered an alternative to your competition at first glance. This will cause your target consumer to engage in your selling proposition. You can see that if this is done well, you'll have many consumers evaluating your selling proposition. If not, you'll suffer the consequences of few consumers evaluating your selling proposition. In that case, how well you have developed your selling proposition will no longer matter.

Before we study real-world examples, consider an exercise that we did for our business that allowed us to view our selling proposition at a glance. We decided that a great demonstration of graphic presentation would be for us to take the selling proposition of The Chambers Group's basic service and apply it to a package as if it were a product that our clients could purchase on a shelf. You can see the result in the following illustration:

If you study it closely you will see that. We have labeled all of the communication elements so you can easily identify them. This exercise has proven valuable for us as we typically communicate our selling proposition in a brochure or in our *Microsoft PowerPoint* capabilities presentation. This allows us to see our entire selling proposition at one glance. We recommend that you,

too, consider putting your selling proposition on the front of a box to see what insights you may gain.

It is always helpful to look at a before and after case study to evaluate the impact that relatively few changes can make in communicating a remarkable selling proposition. To demonstrate this, I have made a series of changes to an Internet business whose homepage is functional to the extent that it is expected to generate revenue. This is not to be confused with the millions of sites that are basically informational. This is an active case study that you can check out for yourself at www.dommusic.com.

Take a look at the following screen capture of the homepage prior to any changes and answer a few pertinent questions. Do you understand the name of the service (the brand), what the product is (the generic descrip-

Brand   Sub-Brand

Endorsement   Attribute   Benefit   Generic
                 Drivers   Descriptor

tor), what you will get out of using it (the benefit) or what the products' features (the attributes) are?

The answers to these questions are: the name is hard to read and I'm not sure what they are selling or what I will get out of using this service. Let's continue by taking a look at the difference that correct changes to these four critical communication elements can make.

Compare the homepage before and after these seemingly simple changes are made.

Notice now that the brand name, SHOCKTRONICA, is easy to read after a simple modification of the letters. At the same time, the character of the logotype is maintained. Even though the name is made up, it can now be read easily and correctly pronounced. It is no longer an obstacle to be overcome. Directly under the brand name you find the generic descriptor that reads "Production Music for Film and Television". Now you know the name of the company and exactly what it does. It provides the music you and I hear while watching a movie or a TV show.

With the fundamental communication now handled, the benefit, "Quick and Easy Licensing", is established as the most powerful way to characterize what the consumers for this business want to get out of using the service. The benefit is intentionally and immediately followed by four attributes that define exactly how it is possible to get the "Quick and Easy Licensing" benefit.

Depending on your personal background or your relationship to the music industry, these words may or may not mean much to you. What is important, however, is that the owner of this website business was smart enough to review the communications model, identify the elements that needed attention and perfect them using terminology his target consumer will understand. It's that simple.

Let's take a look at the *BenGay* package shown here as it relates to the total graphic presentation. At first look the package has a ton of impact achieved by the bright ovoid shape that frames the dark, bold *BenGay* typeface. The target is imme-

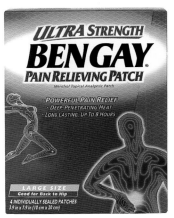

diately aware of the *BenGay* name and the generic descriptor, "Pain Reliev-ing Patch," has been created to communicate the product benefit. The key graphic—the runner icons—targets the product to both men and women. The yellow type in the center of the package is dedicated to listing the prod-uct attributes considered most important.

Overall, we think this is a strong graphic presentation, but offer several tips for improvement. The illustration style and characters in the key graphic are unre-markable and can be found on many other products. Also, a strong endorsement might be valuable to separate this pain relieving patch from all the others. "Origi-nal Strength" is too vague; does this mean the product is stronger or weaker than the one it just replaced? Left to the mind of the consumer ("What's wrong here?"), they'll make the most negative interpretation and possibly not purchase.

No matter what your product or service, you must be extremely careful when updating or restaging an existing selling proposition. These changes might occur yearly as you continually set the pace of evolution in your category. This progression can be applied to any of the positioning elements that make up your selling proposition, including simple changes to your graphic presen-tation. The following are two examples of significant and smart evolutionary changes on the *Cholest Off* and *Triple Flex* products:

 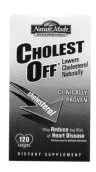  

BEFORE   **AFTER**   **BEFORE**   **AFTER**

Both of these sub-brands are advertised, and perhaps you can see that after the change, they have name recognition after ad exposure making it easier for target consumers to identify them from their commercials. In addition, their selling propositions are more clearly communicated. Their new key graphics, the arrow and the unique treatment of the running man, communicate a great deal about each product. The copy elements are well organized and easy for target consumers to absorb. This is about the maximum change that I would ever recommend.

In the late '70s, I got a call from the marketing VP of a company that had purchased the MJB rice business from *Hills Bros.* coffee company. *Hills Bros.* had purchased it along with MJB's coffee business a few years earlier.

The gentleman came to my office and took an hour to familiarize me with the change that had taken place. Without describing it, I will tell you that his new package design was a significant departure from the previous well-established one. He explained that he had only been with the company for a couple of months, and had inherited the change; it had previously been approved by senior management and launched a few months earlier. He continued to explain the reaction of his target consumers…it was shocking. In the first three months the product had lost more than 60% of its customers. In my lengthy career, that's the worst down slide I've ever heard of.

I was fascinated with the circumstances and agreed to study the problem and get a proposal to him within the week. It didn't take that long. I called him two days later without a proposal and told him that they needed to immediately destroy all the new, unused packages and return to the old design. He reacted with grave disappointment. I told him I was being sincere and did not think any redesign would solve the problem. The target consumer had rejected the new design en masse and needed to see the one they trusted back on the shelf as soon as possible. My recommendation was soundly rejected by his senior managers who considered it a concession.

I agreed that it was, but I also knew that putting their target consumers through a second change would only confuse them more; the only move that they would relate to was a return to what they were comfortable with. In other words, for the first time ever, "unremarkable" was my recommendation.

Looking back, isn't it odd that I would recommend an intentional move from the right side of the paradigm to the left? That is, from the remarkable and apparently very inappropriate to the unremarkable and familiar. After we parted ways, I saw no change on the shelf. I'm sorry to report that the *MJB* rice business has been MIA for some time now. Remember, it's a war out there. They did the right thing in coming to the "hired gun" because they were in big trouble, but had I done what they requested, it would have been the equivalent of throwing myself on their grenade. In my estimation this was one casualty that didn't have to happen—a case of "friendly fire".

The *Cristophe* display unit that follows is a permanent fixture developed to communicate the brand's selling proposition. The impact is achieved by the enlarged photo of *Cristophe* introducing the man responsible for these products. It constitutes a dark area within a light and bright presentation. You will have to look closer [behind the bottles] to discover that he is a "renowned stylist to the stars". The benefit is prominently located in the center of the layout and is rather personal: "Experience Beautiful hair for a more Beautiful you". The reason to believe is accomplished through the 100% guarantee. Lastly,

there is a tag line—"reinventing beauty"—that communicates that the brand is on the "cutting edge". That's probably a good idea as most target consumers of grooming products are open to doing it better.

Overall, we consider this graphic presentation to be strong with the following two suggestions. Consider moving the generic descriptor to a more prominent location. This is a relatively new brand, so few consumers know what its products are just by reading *Cristophe*'s name. We also recommend a unique brand logotype design, which would go a long way toward communicating that these products are also unique.

Being Attractive — People vs. Products

As a wrap-up to this chapter, I'd like to point out that it's helpful to think of your product or service as a person. That's one more way to evaluate the benefit/attribute relationship we covered earlier. It's personal…as it should be.

Ultimately the most powerful benefit works as a reflection of your target consumer. If they can see themselves in your product or service, I guarantee they will buy it. They are not buying your product or service; they are buying an identity enhancer. They are trying to find themselves in things. This quest for self-enhancement is a basic part of human nature. Staying present to this phenomenon will serve you well.

Another context for evaluating the personal aspect of your selling proposition is that you would like your product or service to be attractive to all your target consumers. If you want to be attractive, don't try to be interesting; be interested. You see, "being interesting" is all about you—your product or service—like the attributes we have discussed.

"Interested", on the other hand, is all about them, your target consumers—like the benefits we've discussed. Target consumers are interested in what's in it for them, not you. If you can create and add character that addresses their needs, you are well on your way to becoming perceived as interesting, and therefore, as remarkable.

Let me put it this way—interesting is product or service attribute-oriented; it's like getting ready for a date. You are making yourself as attractive (interesting) as you possibly can, and it's all about the product—you. Certainly some level of attention to product is required, but what about them?

People are so concerned about themselves that they don't know anyone else exists, and aren't going to notice if you're interesting or not. They will, however, be aware of you being interested. So, don't lead with your product attribute no matter how personally involved you are with it or how great you think it is. Lead with them, not you. Be interested in them, the target consumer, not your product. The benefit goes first. This flies in the face of conventional marketing wisdom, which is traditionally centered on talking up the product.

Marketers are so enamored with the characteristics of their products and services that they forget that they are communicating to human beings who want desperately to be acknowledged. Take time to read the labels in your local supermarket, scan the storefronts in your neighborhood and surf the Internet and observe homepages. You'll see what I mean. It's rare that you will find a benefit; they're all too busy talking about themselves. Remember, I never said don't talk about yourself…you must. I just say do it second, not first. Lead with a benefit that addresses the consumer, then drive that benefit to remarkability with an empowering attribute and you will have created one hell of a powerful remarkable trigger.

The good news here is that this scenario is so uncommon in the current marketplace that when you use it effectively, you will devastate your competition.

This is reliable information for you to evaluate how well you are communicating your selling proposition. You can then ask whatever questions you wish, but pay more attention to what you get when giving them very short response times.

Working with Research

Personally, I have no research training in my background nor does anyone on my staff. Nonetheless, we rely heavily on research in two of the three basic stages of developing products and services. The stages I am most familiar with are backgrounding, innovation and validation, in that order.

Background information on the category, including your competition's product history as well as your own, provides a baseline from which to create. Research findings are essential in this effort. In fact, this is the one time when I feel focus groups or interviews are quite valuable. But remember, they're like any other conversation based on asking people what they think; you need to sift through the answers to find the value. It's like asking a political question at a cocktail party—most people like to talk, irrespective of whether they actually have something relevant to say. Humans, in any setting, want to be asked—asked anything. Being asked makes us feel significant. If you think you can't afford professional research, do what one of my sons did when setting up the marketing for a new DVD targeted to infants. He invited eight of his trusted colleagues to dinner in the private room of a local restaurant and led them through a series of questions. It was very productive. They loved being of value in this way, feeling like they had a say in the matter. Smart approach. Even then, you will have to sift carefully through the information you get.

The second phase is innovation, and I know of no research technology that innovates. Innovation is basically a creative function, and listening to target consumers will only give you directional information at best—mostly in the form of complaints. It will always be up to you to create on your target consumers' behalf.

The third phase, validation, can only be accomplished using quantitative research. This type of research is expensive as the research company will have to run it by at least 140 consumers to develop reliable information. Short of a limited test market, it's the only way to validate the concept. It can also provide guidance for tweaking or improving a product or service when internal information provides the "why" behind the target consumer's answers. It is also used to project probable market share and sales volumes. If you are an entrepreneur, you may decide to fly by the seat of your pants, without the research. I can support that.

Do It Yourself

Let me be clear—if you have the funds, hire a professional researcher, tell them you want to learn as much as possible about your target consumer's needs and buying habits, and follow their advice.

If you are short of that kind of funding, I suggest another path. I am going to propose that you consider the possibility that you can create a remarkable selling proposition without the benefit of research or consulting your target consumer in any way. The next chapter is dedicated to showing you exactly how.

The Two Types of Research

Professional marketers spend enormous amounts of money on research. For the most part, research is evaluated as if it always accurately reflects the target consumer's likes and dislikes. Given the sheer volume of research conducted annually, this is unlikely the case.

The research community divides research into two distinct types: qualitative and quantitative.

Qualitative research essentially encompasses the focus groups or one-on-one interviews we have just discussed. Normally, a product or service is exposed to the target consumer and the moderator asks them what they think. As I've said, I rarely ask people what they think, knowing that the answer will usually be made up on the spot and, therefore, likely be inauthentic.

When it comes to this type of research, as I've indicated, you must be careful. Do not submit your ideas for approval; target consumers will easily kill a truly innovative positioning concept.

Quantitative research is based simply on the same question being posed to a large number of target consumers to gather their responses. The quantity needs to be large enough to provide valid results. I am generally comfortable with this form of research as it has, in my experience, proven reliable. In recent years, research companies have made great use of the Internet. The effect is you can reach more people for less cost, further validating your results.

The only way I know of to check the accuracy of research is to redo it. In my experience, however, I know of this happening with only two products in over 20 years. That is how much confidence major brands place on research results. They simply assume it is accurate. I can't help but suspect that that level of trust is often misplaced. Both of the two products I refer to have received very high intent-to-buy scores in the first round and were resubmitted for validation. The unusually high score was considered suspect by the client. Isn't it odd that a good score is more suspect than a poor one? You know the answer to that –"What's wrong?" Researchers are human, too. If a product or service scores poorly, it is typically abandoned and there is no mention of the research being suspect. That dichotomy seems characteristically human to me.

I have one recent example of this scenario. We created a new product for a large East Coast consumer goods manufacturer that, when presented, was met with a lot of excitement. We positioned it carefully, developing many remarkable triggers, then presented it back to the client. They submitted it to an Internet research company with a reliable track record. After waiting two weeks, we were informed that it scored a "C" in all three of the categories in which it was evaluated. That was the only poor score we had been given in years, and so I requested the details of the research.

What I discovered was that the group of target consumers we had worked with was not the same as those used in the research. Knowing the differences between the groups, we reworked the concept and resubmitted it to the client. Two weeks later we got the results of the second test and it scored an "A+" overall. That is the only time in my career that a client allowed us to resubmit a concept to research after it had failed. That product will not likely ever see the light of day though, since the client's major competitor, Procter & Gamble, launched an identical product while we were still in the development phase. It was a great concept, but simply behind its time.

Walk The Walk
Chapter Eleven

Everything I have shared with you up to this point constitutes what I know to be true based upon doing it routinely for others. Along the way it may have occurred to you that I would be a fool not to have applied all I have learned to this book. Great observation…I did, and I'm going to demonstrate it here.

This was my thinking at the time. First, I took a good look at the selling environment…I have never written or sold a book before. The category for *Pull* is the "business books" section of retail and airport bookshops. I had walked through bookstores before without realizing how much they are set up like supermarkets. The big difference, and a large disadvantage, to the bookseller is that the packages are all the same. I realized I would have to do all of my book's positioning with words and graphics where thousands of other books are competing for attention with just as much intention as me.

If you recall Chapter 4, you know I need to accomplish two critical functions or the book will struggle. It must be initially perceived as unique (impact) and then it must immediately communicate a remarkable selling proposition. Let's look at both the front (primary) and back (secondary) covers of the book with those two fundamental tasks in mind. Another fundamental difference is that consumers in a supermarket rarely read beyond the front panel of the package, whereas book buyers normally read both the front and back covers.

For the front cover I chose seven communication elements. You will likely recognize all of them.

IMPACT: If I don't have remarkable impact, consumers will never get to my selling proposition. I must get their attention immediately. The title, *Pull,* is in a black typeface in the center of what is essentially a white book and is designed to work as an attention-getting

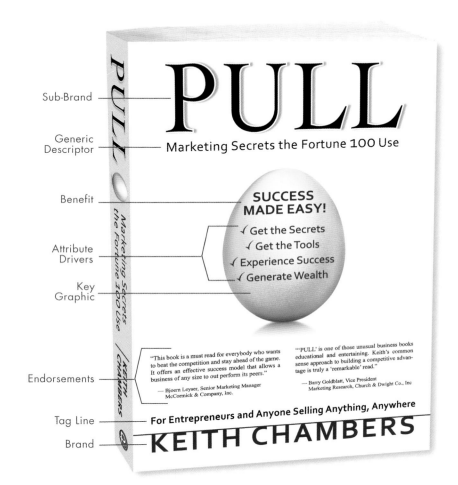

Sub-Brand

Generic
Descriptor

Benefit

Attribute
Drivers

Key
Graphic

Endorsements

Tag Line

Brand

PULL

Marketing Secrets the Fortune 100 Use

SUCCESS
MADE EASY!

✓ Get the Secrets
✓ Get the Tools
✓ Experience Success
✓ Generate Wealth

"This book is a must read for everybody who wants to beat the competition and stay ahead of the game. It offers an effective success model that allows a business of any size to out perform its peers."

— Bjoern Leyser, Senior Marketing Manager
McCormick & Company, Inc.

"'PULL' is one of those unusual business books educational and entertaining. Keith's common sense approach to building a competitive advantage is truly a 'remarkable' read."

— Barry Goldblatt, Vice President
Marketing Research, Church & Dwight Co., Inc

For Entrepreneurs and Anyone Selling Anything, Anywhere

KEITH CHAMBERS

device. Notice the emphasis on the word "Pull" which works as an impact device. Black on white represents 100% contrast—it doesn't get any stronger than that. It also doesn't hurt to have a bull's-eye (golden egg) in the center of the cover.

SUB-BRAND: *Pull*—Given that it is used as the impact, it is clearly the first thing the target consumer will see. It is short, poetic, memorable, and has character that resonates with consumers who may consider it something they do not have. Remember, you are conveying, "I have what you want."

GENERIC DESCRIPTOR: "Marketing Secrets The *Fortune* 100 Use"—Located directly under the sub-brand, it defines what is meant by Pull. The basic generic descriptor is "Marketing Secrets". That clearly defines the book, but in an unremarkable way. I added more… "The *Fortune* 100 Use". Now that is remarkable. Notice how well it works with the sub-brand. So far so good.

BENEFIT: "Success Made Easy!"—is what the target consumer gets out of reading the book. Sounds good, but unremarkable until I empower it with attribute drivers that relate directly to it.

ATTRIBUTE DRIVERS: "Get The Secrets, Get The Tools, Experience Success and Generate Wealth"—The four attribute drivers empower the benefit by answering "how" the benefit is possible. In this book, you get both— the secrets and how to apply them to your business so you can create success for yourself.

KEY GRAPHIC: "The Golden Egg"—Among many other graphics, the golden egg was considered most remarkable. It functions on two levels: 1) as an attention getting device and 2) it communicates wealth.

ENDORSEMENTS: Given that few people outside the world of big business are aware of me, endorsements are important. There are two here, four on the back cover and eight on the inside first pages.

TAG LINE: "For Entrepreneurs, Marketers & CEOs"—I chose this

$19.95 U.S./$21.57 Can.

Benefit

SUCCESS MADE EASY...

Attribute Copy

"If you are currently selling anything, then you are engaged in an all-out economic war. If you are among those who don't believe this, you are likely to become one of its casualties." These are the sobering words of Keith Chambers, a high-level marketing consultant for America's Fortune 100 brands. Within this community he is commonly referred to as "a hired marketing gun," a reference he loves.

This book is the result of Chambers recreating his remarkable "big business" marketing methodology for small and medium-size businesses. If you are one of those, then you picked up the right book. Here, you will not only discover his strategy, you will also find his detailed methodology for implementing it into your business, and in turn, into your life. Your competition will be devastated.

Endorsements

"'PULL' offers a concise, easy-to-understand path to successful marketing – whether it's a service, product, or even yourself."
—Christine Yau, Market Research Manager, LifeScan / Johnson & Johnson

"A winning process that challenges you to use the consumer in a unique way! It brings together consumer input and creativity like never before."
—Deborah Breivogel, Senior Manager Market Research, Schering-Plough, Claritin

"'PULL' reads like a fast pace novel and teaches lessons with immediate results which continue to produce exponentially through the years."
—George F. Bauer, Former President/CEO of the Miss America Organization

"Finally, an insider's guide to marketing secrets that the big boys use. This 'how to' book on positioning introduces marketers and business owners to *an easy to follow* methodology developed and refined in the marketplace... and proven at the cash register".
—Archie J. Thornton, Former Managing Director of Ogilvy & Mather Worldwide

ISBN: 978-0-9768617-7-5

51995

9 780976 861775

PULL

Marketing Secrets the Fortune 100 Use | KEITH CHAMBERS

line to let target consumers know whom the book applies to simply because it seemed important.

BRAND: In this case, I am the brand. Given I am not a household name, I chose to subordinate it.

For the back cover I chose four communication elements. You will likely recognize all of these as well:

BENEFIT: SUCCESS MADE EASY. This is the same benefit as that on the front cover. It is repeated here as a lead into the more detailed explanation of the attributes that are seen on the front cover.

ATTRIBUTE COPY: This copy is an expansion of all the attribute drivers on the front cover egg. It introduces the author in a dramatic way and characterizes the contents of the book.

ENDORSEMENTS: These are in addition to the front cover endorsements, all of which are considered essential to building credibility.

There you have it. I will leave it to you to judge.

Creative Preparation
Chapter Twelve

Before we jump into the task of creating a new or revised selling proposition for your business, let's look at a few distinctions that will make the process easier.

Creating "What's Next?"

Developing remarkable triggers is clearly a creative function. The future of your business is hanging on your creativity and your awareness. How creative are you on a scale of 1 to 10? Let's say that 1 is "not creative at all" and 10 is "as creative as the creative director at a major advertising agency". Pause and think for a moment before you read on. Pick a number.

I frequently ask large groups this question and the number of people who answer "10" is approximately 1 out of 20. That is consistent for most demographic groups except one. If I am working with teens, it is about 1 in 30. Teens, I have noticed are unexpectedly quiet and not very expressive when asked to respond creatively. I think they are at a stage where they are confronted with life and are therefore generally suppressed.

This is my experience on how creative you are. That goes for you no matter what demographic group you belong to. I've been well paid over the years to be accountable for being creative. I can tell you without exception that all of you are just as creative as I am. There is a reason you did not consider yourself a 10 the instant I asked the question. You were born a 10 and then something happened. Think back to when you were around seven or eight and see if this sounds familiar.

One day you were outside playing in the mud. You cleverly created something, maybe a pirate ship out of mud and sticks. You were so excited about your creation that you ran into the house to show your mom. "Mom, look at my pirate ship," you said. Mom had just finished cleaning the house and responded in kind: "Get that out of the house, now!" You were crushed, and in that moment, you went from a 10 to a 9. Then, on your way out the door, you showed your older brother the ship. He pointed at it, laughed, and called you an idiot. Being your brother, he went even further—he threatened to tell your friends that you were a moron. After he got through, you lowered yourself to an 8. Chances are you continued to adjust downward based upon other similar experiences until it settled where it is today.

From that day forward, you suppressed your creative side because people were not listening to you that way. You created some other expertise to replace it. You have been telling yourself that you are that number for so long that it has become reality for you. Today, right now, I invite you to take responsibility for being a 10, because you are.

Tattoos Are "Cool"

I recommend you get a tattoo. You should have the word "pull" etched in a prominent place. I will leave its exact location up to you. Just make sure it works as a constant reminder. In time, it should become a permanent part of your psyche—only then you can have the tattoo removed.

For a time, one of my sons had the name "Gandhi" across the top of his computer. It became his personal truing principle. The presence of that word made such a difference in who he is in his business life that he recently replaced it with a tattoo of Buddha on his shoulder. Knowing my son as I do, he did not do it because he thought it was cool. For him, it functions as a constant reminder of his own truing principle and it serves as a significant contributor to his success.

On my computer I have—you guessed it—"pull". I am confronted with it daily. You will be, too. It may not be as inspirational as "Gandhi", but it works for me. Here is an example of how insidious pull is. Check yourself right now. How many times during the reading of this book have you read something I have said and compared it to what you already know, or said something in your head to make what I said unremarkable? Let's face it, there's a good likelihood that you have been trying to drag every one of the insights you have gotten from this book back to the left side of the paradigm. You compare them to what you already know and discount them. That's human nature. You're wired to reduce the significance of anything that comes along so you can deal with it; that's how you keep yourself comfortable. Don't berate yourself for doing it, just remember that it is how humans make everything okay. All of us. If your awareness of it fades, you are at risk as a marketer. Okay. You really don't have to get a tattoo. I was simply trying to communicate how pervasive this "pull" really is and how intentional you will have to be to avoid it. It's up to you to create your own way of staying present to it. Be creative and invent your own personal reminder. Have fun with it.

Success Is Labor Intensive

This is where learning what "pull" is may get you into trouble. If it becomes part of your intelligence, you will lose it quickly. If you let that happen, pull will get you and you won't even know it. It will get filed away with the rest of your knowledge and be of no value. This is where you want to become and stay aware of it or it will get you. Can you see the difference? It will take a great deal of rigor to do that; and most people don't have the rigor it takes. You will need to keep the remarkability paradigm in mind and periodically ask yourself whenever you make a decision: "Is what we have just decided on the left (unremarkable) or right (remarkable) side of the paradigm?"

In my business life, I have noticed a direct correlation between success and rigor. I can tell you that success is labor intensive. There are few examples to the contrary.

The definition of rigor for this purpose is "severity in dealing with something." Without a great deal of rigor relative to the distinction "pull", you will create on the left side of the paradigm and think you are on the right side. Are you capable of the rigor that is required? Have you ever experienced the need to be rigorous?

I Learned Rigor

As my career in the Air Force advanced, I was asked to learn to pilot an aircraft that was capable of flying at higher altitudes where a pressurized cockpit was typically required. I was assigned an aircraft that was an exception as it was not pressurized. The lack of pressurization was handled by installing a pressurized oxygen system. What that meant was that the pilot was subjected to pure oxygen under pressure at altitudes above 20,000 feet.

"Under pressure" are the operative words here. That means when you relax the air rushes into your lungs instead of out. Breathing becomes a new experience. In order to fly the mission, it was necessary to acclimate to this new way of breathing so it would become routine. In all of the time that I flew that aircraft, I do not know of a pilot who was able to do it with ease. Rigor was the order of the day. I had to stay aware of my breathing in order to function in the mission. Breathing had nothing to do with the mission, yet it was impossible to ignore that aspect. I had to think about breathing constantly, otherwise I would hyperventilate and be unable to perform the mission. The rigor required to stay aware of "pull" is no less critical. You will have to function and make marketing decisions and stay aware of "pull" or it will get you. The penalty for losing your awareness is unremarkability. In other words, get the tattoo.

When Hope Replaces Rigor

Thinking that things are going to change for the better without committed action is called hope. When hope is accompanied by rigor I am all for it. However, the hope I am referring to is the hope that often occurs and replaces rigor. That hope is basically worthless, and I recommend you avoid that hope at all cost. If you are in hope, you are not in action. Not being in action guarantees you are in the hands of others. That may work out every once in a while, but why not take charge and make something happen?

Are you a Yankees fan? Simply watch a game at home and hope like hell that the Yankees win. You'll discover that win or lose, you'll experience a great deal of frustration. For the next game, go to the ballpark and yell your heart out so that you may literally affect the outcome of the game. Not only is being in action good business, it's good therapy.

If you look even closer at hope, you will see the implication of waiting for something to occur, typically something positive. In the marketing war, waiting will get you wounded or killed. Can you imagine standing in line in the middle of a battlefield? It's done routinely in the world of free enterprise. I can think of no context in which waiting has any value; for me, it has always been painful. I got that training early in my life on that same golf course in Ohio where my career first…well, ignited.

Looking back at my career as a ball hound, I recall it blossomed over a period of years until around age 14, when I had risen to the job of caddy master. The caddy master is the kid who manages the caddies and also runs the pro shop when the pro is away.

Every Monday, our pro was off attending Pro-Am tournaments at different courses around the state. So on Mondays, I was responsible for opening the pro shop in the morning and selling small items to members until closing time at dusk.

On a slow day toward the end of summer, I was supervising one of the caddies who was cleaning clubs. It was one of those balmy afternoons when boredom sets in and good judgment takes leave. Absurd thoughts somehow seem rational at such a moment. The pro had given us a bucket of a new solution to clean the clubs with and, in doing so, informed me that the cleaner was flammable so I should be careful with it. Perhaps he did not realize he was talking to a 14-year-old idiot.

At one point, one of the caddies came up to me and announced that he had spilled a large amount of the new solution on the wood floor in the back. In that moment, I decided that the best way to clean it up was to clear out the area and throw a match on the spill; I figured that would just burn it away. Looking back, I am less puzzled by the abject stupidity of the idea than I am by the fact that it came to me seemingly without any thought to the possible consequences. Well, I was only 14, but I still don't recognize that person as myself.

The result will come as no surprise. In seconds, the flames were six feet high and that area of the pro shop was getting hot. I ran outside with the empty bucket to a water spigot and tried desperately to fill it. It seemed to take forever as I could only watch through the window as my caddy accomplice was beating the flames with a towel.

After two buckets of water, I was only able to slow the fire down, so we began pulling as many of the members' clubs out of the building as we could. Within the hour, the fire was out thanks to someone having called the fire department, but over half of the building was gutted.

I remember vividly sitting outside the charred building in the only remaining chair for hours waiting for the pro to return. There I was, waiting and hoping. I really was an idiot. It was a gut-wrenching experience as I tried in vain to create a scenario that would reasonably explain what had happened. I mean, not what had happened but what I had done. In my misery, all I was able to do was hope for the best. I was locked in hope and waiting. That miserable experience remains with me today. Waiting and hoping–absolutely worthless.

Since that time, there has been no waiting in my life to match that waiting, or hope to match that hope. Both waiting and hope of any kind were forever altered for me. I assume the same is true for you.

Looking back, I know that fire provided a profound lesson, but I could have handled it in a way that would have been less painful. As you read on I will distinguish the value of being in action. Today with cell phones, that distinction would have had me call the pro and share what had happened as soon as the waiting started. That would have minimized the suffering by shortening it. If one must suffer, and we must, I am all for short suffering. If he had fired me in that moment over the phone, the agony would have stopped. As it occurred, he fired me when he arrived. However, even had cell phones been around in those days, I doubt I would have had the insight at that age to make the call and shorten the suffering.

Great References

In the back of the book, on pages 214 through 217, you will find the Nu Stuff package, the Shocktronica homepage, the *SeaTales* email flyer and the cover of this book. I have identified and labeled all of the communication elements on each. Where I have done so, you may assume that I consider each a remarkable trigger. It will be useful for you to refer these examples as you work with your own selling proposition. You can copy them or simply tear them out of the book for reference.

Backgrounding

Backgrounding is very important. You are likely to assume that you are aware of all that is going on within the reach of your category, but I encourage you to assume nothing. The dynamic of the marketplace is cause for new circumstances on almost a daily basis. If you are prudent, you will want to stay current.

Keep the glossary close by and get comfortable with the terminology. When you run into a term that defines something significant to your business, you may want to return to that section of the book and review it thoroughly. You will want to collect information on the category you are competing in. You will want to evaluate your competition with emphasis on how each competitor functions in your category. Study their successes and failures as well as each of their strengths and weaknesses. This information will stimulate your thinking and will have you function more aggressively.

Applying This to Your Business
Chapter Thirteen

At this point I recommend you consider three courses of action, any one of which is absolutely appropriate. You will make your choice based on the condition of your business, the availability of your time and your ability and willingness to ask others to assist you in the work ahead. Whichever you choose, it is my commitment that this book provide you the means to do so.

1) The Team Approach—Your first choice is to follow the team approach that I have constructed for those of you who want to devote the time and energy to pursue the optimum application of this work. It is a bit rigorous, very much like the process we use daily for our clients. This process is detailed and since it involves target consumers, you will need to allow time for it to unfold. This is not something that you should do quickly. Our experience is that if you take your time and work the process carefully, the changes you will make will devastate your competition.

2) Do It Yourself—Your second choice is to take immediate action to create the options and make the choices necessary to drive your business forward now. To do so, I recommend you take a modified approach to the step-by-step team procedure I have developed and present just ahead. The modification I am referring to is based on you proceeding through the recommended steps to position or reposition your business, but you will do it on your own. The process is set up for you to involve target consumers, but in this scenario, you will do the process without them. If you choose to do so, you will reap powerful results simply based on the abstractions and distinctions that you now command. As you follow the detailed process you will simply skip that portion of the work allocated for your teammates. This work is detailed and though you will want quick results, I caution against "racing" through the pro-

cess. Upon completion, given you have taken the time to work the process properly, you will have made great changes and will see positive
results soon after implementation.

3) Good To Go—Your third choice is based on the fact that you
are now in possession of a great deal of information that will change
how you run your business and likely generate more success for
yourself without any need for immediate action. Over time, and as
issues arise you will reference sections of the book that will serve
to guide you and influence the choices you make. Continuing to do
so will significantly benefit your business. If this is your choice, you
can rest in the comfort of knowing that you are well ahead of your
competition. You may want to read ahead for additional insights
even if you choose not to do the additional work.

My recommendation is for you to choose which of these three feels the most
comfortable. You may choose all three over time by working your way into the
process slowly. Whatever your choice, you are way ahead of your competition.

Scope

Scope essentially defines how large a project is. It identifies all of the work
to be done. Establishing scope is accomplished by reviewing the Communications Model (page 212) and selecting the positioning elements you are
going to work on. This process is simple. You will use the communications
model in the back of the book, and methodically review each element, one
by one, and choose those you think have potential for creating remarkable
triggers. The Communications Model has 15 elements for you to consider.
In over fifteen years of working with this document, I have never selected
all of the elements for any one project. You will most likely choose from
five to seven that are important to your business and those will constitute
the scope of your positioning project. If you are creating a new business
you will likely choose more than if you are repositioning an existing business. If you have an existing business you will want to consider a sub-
brand, but keep in mind, very few brands have the need for a sub-brand.

From this point forward, those elements not chosen become irrelevant.

You now have the knowledge and the tools required to develop a remarkable selling proposition for your business and you have identified the scope of the task to do so. You will soon discover that your awareness of the material in this book will give you a higher level of confidence in the choices you make while routinely conducting your business.

The Procedure—Part I

What follows has been developed for those of you who are inspired to rework your current selling proposition, as well as for those of you who are in the process of launching a new business. For those of you who have nothing to run through the process at this time, I suggest you read on as there is a great deal more to be learned here. I have created a step-by-step procedure that will guide you through the process in an orderly and effective way. It is exactly how I would do it if I were an entrepreneur with little or no marketing help.

Creating success happens when you work with the remarkability paradigm and the communications model. Given their importance, let's review the fundamentals and, most importantly, how they work together.

Up to this point, you have been recording your observations and insights in the back of the book (page 213) and gaining a sense of what action you can take to move your business forward. I am going to recommend that you use what you have created up to this point as a base from which to rethink all of what you've learned. If you choose to be aggressive, the team approach will work for you. There is nothing more powerful than a small team of inspired people aligned in their goals and aware of the insights that make it possible to achieve them. The team will have at least three players, including you. You absolutely do not need more, but if you prefer a larger team do not go over a total of six. You will find that five teammates is a lot to deal with. It will be important to use your teammates carefully. Keep their workload simple and use them only for the most important feedback. I have developed the methodology that follows with the thought of keeping it easy for your teammates. My assumption for the remainder of this chapter is that you are going to recruit and work with teammates. If you are the do-it-yourselfer, simply follow the team process as I referenced earlier, by improvising where teammates are recommended.

You have noticed by now that I have used the word team many times when referring to a group of people working on one project within a large company. I also used it in Chapter 5 when referring to my having a small team of friends. That team was created specifically to share business and marketing related ideas on a continuing basis. The team I want you to assemble now is a bit different. Your team should be made up of target consumers. Your target consumers are for the most part, the only opinions that matter. You may have to interview a few before confirming your team but it should be relatively easy to find two, and that is all you need. Two calls are required.

The first is a call with each prospect individually. We refer to this call as an enrollment conversation and it has four topics to be covered in the following order:

- Acknowledge their friendship and share your respect for their business judgment.

- Briefly share what you are about to take on in your business.

- Request their limited yet critical participation in the process.

- Explain that they can count on you devoting as much time back to them in the future if ever needed.

- Explain that they will be exposed to an extraordinary marketing process.

- Explain that they will be required to sign a release for all that gets created in the process. This is a necessity. Do not, under any circumstances, work in this way with anyone who has not signed this document. That includes relatives and fiancés too. The release is a simple document that you will be able to find on any of the websites that specialize in legal and business forms such as www.legalzoom.com…there are others.

- Explain that they will be compensated for their participation in the process. I recommend their compensation be in the form of goods or services from your business, if possible. You will be bartering for their services. Additionally, I recommend you give them perks as the work progresses. You can start with *Starbucks* or other coupons. It is not necessary that you spend a lot of money. This is an acknowledgement of their contribution to you and your business that is important so they don't feel taken advantage of. The tip here is to use the coupons as an unanticipated extra so your teammates will remain engaged.

The second call is a conference call that you will set at a time that works for all of your teammates. Even if you have to wait a bit to get it scheduled, it is important for all of you to start together. This can also be accomplished in a meeting or a dinner, if your teammates are located close. You will give them two props to refer to:

- An outline document that you will create. This document identifies each point you will cover while explaining the nature of your business to them. This is your history, your aspirations for the future and lastly a review of the positioning elements on the communications model (page 212) that you intend to work with. Have the glossary close by to provide simple definitions for the terminology you are likely to use.

- The Remarkability Paradigm (page 211). You will explain it in more abbreviated language than I did, with emphasis on its three critically important distinctions…remarkability, pull and appropriate.

The Procedure—Part II

Now that you have worked with your team to identify the positioning elements you are going to use, you will follow the procedure outlined while guiding your team through the process element by element. Although it is very unlikely that you have chosen all fifteen elements, I am going to advise you on how to approach all of them. I am also going to give you specific words to use when you request input from your teammates. I will do that in blue so it is easy to distinguish it from the instructions I am laying out for you. You will need to adjust your teammate instructions slightly to specifically identify your type of business. Simply rewrite what I have given you here. You and your teammates are going to address your chosen elements one by one until you have completed all the exercises. You will notice that I have slightly changed the order of the elements from that in the communications model (page 212). I have done so to accommodate the special relationships that exist between several of the elements. Those relationships will become evident as you work your way through the process.

One last note before you begin: If you are repositioning an existing business, I recommend you always include the positioning element you are currently using, if one exists. For example, if you are working on creating possible new benefits and you are already using a benefit, be sure to include your current benefit at the beginning of the exercise. If it should turn out to be the strongest, you will simply keep using it. If you are a do-it-yourselfer, you will simply ignore those places where I refer to working with your teammates. For those of you who are working with target consumers, simply follow my instructions and you will be successful. Irrespective of which group you belong to, be sure not to rush the process and it will work.

The Process

Generic Descriptor

FIRST: Explain in person or send an email to each of your teammates requesting they create six possible generic descriptors for your business using the following guideline (you too will do the exercise). You will use the definitions I provide here, with one exception. If your business is in the category I chose when creating the example you will need to create new examples that are outside your category.

TEAMMATE REQUEST:

MY BUSINESS DEFINITION: (EXAMPLE: A retail dry cleaning store).

GENERIC DESCRIPTOR DEFINITION: It defines my product or service exactly as it is in no more than four words.

EXAMPLE—"Dry Cleaning"

Please create four total generic descriptors for my business based upon the definitions above and my previous discussions with you, and send them back to me. The first two should define my business exactly as it is with no embellishments. Both should be from two to four words… no more.

To create the second two, simply add one or two words at most to each of the first two. These added words should characterize my business and complement the first two generic descriptors you created.

If YOGURT is a good generic descriptor, then adding PORTA-BLE, "Portable Yogurt" or PLAYFUL, "Playful Yogurt" is a good example.

SECOND: Once you receive your teammates' responses you will have at least 12 to work with. You can expect that some of them will be very much alike. That is the nature of them being generic. This includes your four as well. You will use what you know about generic descriptors to choose your top three. You may want to reread the generic descriptor section of the book. Having done so, either sit down with or send the top three back to your team-mates with the following instructions.

TEAMMATE REQUEST:

MY BUSINESS DEFINITION: (EXAMPLE; A retail dry cleaning store).

GENERIC DESCRIPTOR DEFINITION: It defines my product or

service exactly as it is in no more that four words.

EXAMPLE: —"Dry Cleaning"

Below are the top three generic descriptors being considered for my business. Please rank order them 1 through 3, with 1 being the best and send them back to me. Base your ranking on their accurately defining my business exactly as it is with an even higher ranking for those that add additional character to the definition. The result must not be at all confusing.

GENERIC DESCRIPTOR	GENERIC DESCRIPTOR
GENERIC DESCRIPTOR	

THIRD: Upon receiving your teammates' responses, you will evaluate them and choose the one that you feel most aligns itself with the objectives described in the generic descriptor section of the book. Be mindful that if you have only two teammates they may not perfectly agree, in which case you will choose the one you feel is best based upon your experience. You can have confidence in your decision irrespective of their response, as you are working with the best of the best at this point. The generic descriptor you choose will now be used in the Brand/Sub-Brand exercise that follows.

Brand or Sub-Brand

FIRST: Explain or send an email to each of your teammates requesting they create eight possible brand/sub-brand names for your business using the following guidelines (you, too, will do this exercise).

TEAMMATE REQUEST:

MY BUSINESS DEFINITION: (EXAMPLE; A retail dry cleaning store).

BRAND/SUB-BRAND DEFINITION: It characterizes the product

or service in a way that stimulates immediate target consumer interest. It does not have to define the product in any way. The generic descriptor did that.

EXAMPLE: —"Carriage Trade"

Please create EIGHT possible brand/sub-brand names based upon the definitions above and my previous discussions with you, and send them back to me. Do so by following the three steps below, which will make the process relatively easy. You can use a printed thesaurus but if you have a computer I suggest you use the *Microsoft Word* thesaurus as indicated below.

1) Create a list of words, some of which characterize my business and others that characterize yourself the target consumer. Using *Microsoft Word*, open the "tools" bar and click on Thesaurus. One by one, enter all of your words. As you do, it will list synonyms. Scan the synonyms list and add those to your list that you think have the potential. After adding a word, you will next highlight and click on the word that will in-turn create a new list of synonyms for that word. Continue that path until you run out of good words, then enter the next word on your initial list. Chances are you will have a significant list when you have finished. When you are done, if you had a dry cleaning business, your list might look like the following:

STYLE	APPEARANCE
CLASS	CHIC
IMAGE	SHARP
LOOKS	VOGUE

2) Now work with the words you have created by adding additional words in front or behind them that add even more character. For example, if you had created the above list you might add to it as indicated below:

NEW LOOK	IN STYLE
STYLE IT	FIRST CLASS
L A LOOKS	IMAGE ONE

Please choose the eight that you feel add character to my business, remembering that it is not at all necessary to define the business and send them back to me. That function is the responsibility of the generic descriptor.

SECOND: Once you have received all responses from your team, including yours, you will have at least 24. You will evaluate them based upon what you learned in the brand section of the book with the goal of narrowing them down to the top three. In doing so you will need to check to ensure that they are legally available.

Checking the availability of brand/sub-brand names is standard practice in the corporate marketing world as they develop new products or services. This is easy to do, and costs NO money. You simply check and see which of the brand/sub-brand names already have trademarks. Names that already have trademarks in your category of business should not be used. You should do this as you are narrowing down to your final three so you are not chasing names that you will not be able to use. The following URL will take you to a website that is designed for this purpose. http://www.uspto.gov/

Once you have chosen the name you want to use, I further recommend you consult a trademark attorney with all of your search materials in hand to get a final, more thorough search and apply for legal protection.

You most likely now have between 5 and 10 names left after the others have been legally disqualified. If you lost all, or only have a couple names left that you are not thrilled about, you are going to have to repeat the process. If so, do not be discouraged, it happens to us too. You are probably not adding words that have a lot of character to your initial words. You are being too generic. You may be trying to describe your business. If so, you are expe-

MY BUSINESS DEFINITION: (EXAMPLE; I sell sandpaper).

ATTRIBUTE DEFINITION: There are two kinds of attributes: 1– is a physical characteristic of my product or service (what is in it or what it's made of), and 2– is a performance characteristic of my product or service (what it does in the performance of its function).

EXAMPLE: SANDPAPER—"Cuts Three Times Faster," "Won't Clog"

Below are the top eight attributes being considered for my business. Each appears with the top benefit that was previously selected. Please rank order them 1 through 8, with 1 being the best and send them back to me. Base your ranking on how well each attribute supports my benefit.

BENEFIT	BENEFIT	BENEFIT	BENEFIT
Attribute #1	Attribute #2	Attribute #3	Attribute #4
BENEFIT	BENEFIT	BENEFIT	BENEFIT
Attribute #5	Attribute #6	Attribute #7	Attribute #8

SECOND: Once you have received all responses, you will evaluate them based upon what you learned in the attribute section of the book and choose the three you feel are most important to your target consumers, and send them back to your teammates using the following guideline.

TEAMMATE REQUEST:

MY BUSINESS DEFINITION: (EXAMPLE; I sell sandpaper).

ATTRIBUTE DEFINITION: There are two kinds of attributes: 1– is a physical characteristic of my product or service (what is in it or what it's made of), and 2– is a performance characteristic of my product or service (what it does in the performance of its function).

EXAMPLE: SANDPAPER—"Cuts Three Times Faster," "Won't Clog"

Below are the top three attributes being considered for my business.

Each appears with the top benefit that we previously selected. Please rank order them 1 through 3, with 1 being the best and send them back to me. Base your ranking on how well each one of them supports my benefit.

BENEFIT	BENEFIT	BENEFIT
Attribute #1	Attribute #2	Attribute #3

THIRD: Upon receiving your teammates' responses, you will evaluate them and choose the two that you feel most align themselves with the objectives described in the attribute section of the book. Be mindful that if you have only two teammates they may not agree, in which case you will have to choose the one you feel is best based upon your experience. You can have confidence in your decision irrespective of their response, as you are working with the best of the best at this point.

Tag Line

FIRST: Explain in person or send an email to each of your teammates requesting they create two possible tag lines for your business using the following guideline (you, too, will do the exercise).

TEAMMATE REQUEST:

MY BUSINESS DEFINITION: (EXAMPLE; I sell suntan lotion.)

TAG LINE DEFINITION: A sweeping statement that dramatizes a key feature of my product or service. It acts as an elaborate benefit statement.

EXAMPLE: SUNTAN LOTION—"Tan safely while nurturing your skin"

Please create two tag lines for my business based upon the definitions above and my previous discussions with you and send them back to me.

EXAMPLE: JEWELRY— "Different styles of earrings", "Different styles of necklaces"

Below are three different configurations of my earrings that are being considered for my business. Please rank them form 1 to 3 with 1 being best based on your interest in purchasing them.

PRODUCT #1   PRODUCT #2   PRODUCT #3

SECOND: Upon receiving your teammates' responses, you will evaluate them and choose the configuration of your product or service that you feel most aligns itself with the objectives of your business. Be mindful that if you have only two teammates they may not agree, in which case you will have to choose the one you feel is best based upon your experience. You can have confidence in your decision irrespective of their response, as you are working with the best of the best at this point.

Container Configuration

FIRST: This exercise is specifically for those of you who are marketing products. If you're selling a service you will skip the next three exercises. In this section the creatively in your hands because you are intimately familiar with the characteristics of your business, and your teammates are not. You will need to take the time to identify (three to five) container options that you feel are appropriate and have the potential to be perceived as remarkable by your target consumers. I suggest you go back to the product configuration section in Chapter 9 and review it. If you have employees, you can ask them to create container options as well. They will probably come up with a couple that you may have missed. You will have to use your knowledge of containers and container suppliers to identify as many possibilities as possible. You will create a graphic depiction (illustration or photograph) of your options that is appropriate for evaluation by your teammates. Having done so, send three to five choices to your teammates using the following guideline:

TEAMMATE REQUEST:

MY BUSINESS DEFINITION: (EXAMPLE; I sell custom jewelry.)

CONTAINER CONFIGURATION DEFINITION: The specific nature of the container that will house and display my product.

EXAMPLE: JEWELRY— A folding carton with a window or a plastic see through package.

Below are three different packaging options for my earrings that are being considered for my business. Please rank them from 1 to 3 with 1 being best based on your interest in purchasing them.

PACKAGE #1	PACKAGE #2	PACKAGE #3

SECOND: Upon receiving your teammates' responses, you will evaluate them and choose the container configuration that you feel most aligns itself with the objectives of your business. Be mindful that if you have only two teammates they may not agree, in which case you will have to choose the one you feel is best based upon your experience. You can have confidence in your decision irrespective of their response, as you are working with the best of the best at this point.

Product Presentation

FIRST: This exercise is specifically for those of you who are marketing products. In this section the creatively in your hands because you are intimately familiar with the characteristics of your business, and your teammates are not. You will need to take the time to identify (three to five) product presentation options that you feel are appropriate and have the potential to be perceived as remarkable by your target consumers. Your package is the impact point for this and you have two options. You can show it through a window or you can depict it graphically printed on the front of the package. You also have the option of not showing it at all which is appropriate in many categories such as perfume. I suggest you go back to the product presentation section in Chapter 9 and review it. If you have employees, you can ask them to create graphic presentation options as well. They will probably come up with a couple that you may have missed. You will create your options and apply them to packages. I recommend you limit the graphics that accompany your product presentation options. Consider that you only use your Brand name, generic descriptor, your benefit and two attribute drivers. Having done so you will photograph each and send three to five choices to your teammates using the following guideline. One option to consider is no depiction of the product.

TEAMMATE REQUEST:

MY BUSINESS DEFINITION: (EXAMPLE; I sell lip gloss for teenage girls.)

PRODUCT PRESENTATION DEFINITION: The graphic or the physical depiction of your product.

EXAMPLE: *Grins N' Giggles* lip gloss. A close up of teen lips. A close up of the product and applicator. No picture at all.

Below are three different packages that display my product differently. They are all being considered for my business. Please rank them from 1 to 3 with 1 being best based on your interest in purchasing them.

PACKAGE #1	PACKAGE #2	PACKAGE #3

SECOND: Upon receiving your teammates' responses, you will evaluate them and choose the product presentation that you feel most aligns itself with the objectives of your business. Be mindful that if you have only two teammates they may not agree, in which case you will have to choose the one you feel is best based upon your experience. You can have confidence in your decision irrespective of their response, as you are working with the best of the best at this point.

Delivery System

FIRST: This exercise is specifically for those of you who are marketing products. In this section the creatively in your hands because you are intimately familiar with the characteristics of your business, and your teammates are not. You will need to take the time to identify (three to five) delivery system options that you feel are appropriate and have the potential to be perceived as remarkable by your target consumers. I suggest you go back to the product configuration section in Chapter 9 and review it. If you have employees, you can ask them to create container options as well. They will probably come up with a couple that you may have missed. You will have to use your knowledge of containers and container suppliers to identify as many possibilities as possible. You will create a graphic depiction (illustration or photograph) of your options that is appropriate for evaluation by your teammates. Typically a delivery system is a package that is functional in some way which sets it aside from a standard container. Having done so, send three to five choices to your teammates using the following guideline:

TEAMMATE REQUEST:

MY BUSINESS DEFINITION: (EXAMPLE; I sell candy.)

DELIVERY SYSTEM DEFINITION: A container that has a function that goes beyond simply housing it.

EXAMPLE: *PEZ* candy— A plastic container that dispenses the product in addition to housing and protecting it.

Below are three different packaging delivery systems options for my earrings that are being considered for my business. Please rank them from 1 to 3 with 1 being best based on the strength of your interest in purchasing them.

DELIVERY SYSTEM #1	DELIVERY SYSTEM #2
DELIVERY SYSTEM #3	

SECOND: Upon receiving your teammates' responses, you will evaluate them and choose the delivery system that you feel most aligns itself with the objectives of your business. Be mindful that if you have only two teammates they may not agree, in which case you will have to choose the one you feel is best based upon your experience. You can have confidence in your decision irrespective of their response, as you are working with the best of the best at this point.

Once you begin work on your selling proposition, you will be called upon to create ideas and make choices irrespective of whether you choose to use teammates or not. Just ahead, I offer coaching on both of those tasks.

Making Critical Choices

From this point forward, you will be working without the team so I recommend you take the time to acknowledge your teammates. I recommend you do so in writing and consider giving them an additional small gift.

You are now going to work on each element one at a time as you incorporate them into your graphic presentation. While doing so you are staying present to the fact that character creates remarkability. You are not necessarily stuck with the winner in each element. You will use your good judgment to consider the first and second place winners, and choose what combination of words and graphics best fit together to form the most powerful overall communication. Watch out for advice from people outside your team. In fact, it's a good idea to set a policy of no suggestions at all. Any advice you get will come to you from the left side of the paradigm and you know that's not powerful. Trust that you now have the correct insights.

This is a great time for you to reference the examples on pages 214 through 217. Remember that your target consumer is probably more willing to be playful in challenging your product or service than you are—in adding significant character—whereas you are pulled to being more literal and in turn more unremarkable. You may have to catch up to them. Push yourself out into "What's next?" Many of you will be repositioning your existing business, and need to be aware of the risk of being too conservative in making the change.

The Conservative Choice

If you are restaging an existing product or service, you need to watch out for another common trap. It concerns the magnitude of the change that your target consumers are going to experience. Obviously, a radical change will not work. That would push the product into a scenario similar to a new product introduction. That hazard is obvious, and this mistake is not likely to happen.

The concern, however, is that if you get too conservative, you may make too small of a change. A small change sounds safe, but it's not. If you make a change that's too small, you're forcing your current target consumer to rethink you without attracting new prospects to your new selling proposition. This is extremely risky. You must make enough of a change to cause the category non-users to reconsider you. Having done so, you will need

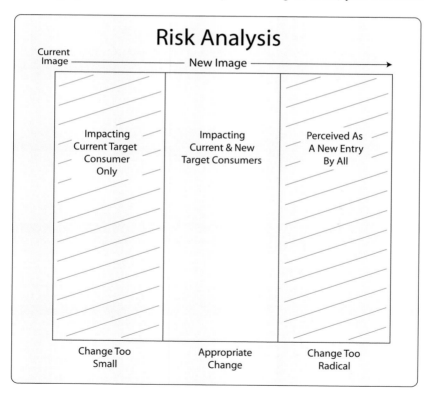

to cross-check that you have not alienated your current target consumer by becoming inappropriate. There is only one circumstance when I recommend a conservative change, and that is, as I just explained, where you are tweaking an established product to accommodate the launch of a new one. Otherwise, never make a small change.

Following are three *Nature's Resource* packages that represent two evolutionary changes in the brand's graphic presentation. The first change, from the package on the left to the package in the center, took place in 2002. It is significant in the organization of the positioning elements, yet the information is essentially the same. There are a number of improvements from the round green panel that serves as a key graphic to the improved legibility of the brand and product names. This change is clearly important enough to appeal to all category users, yet retains enough of the cap, bottle and label color, combined with the strong brand name presentation, so that it's easy enough for current users to identify.

The change from the center bottle to the one on the right took place in 2008. This transformation was designed to accommodate the change from the *Nature's Resource* to the *Nature Made* brand. This is also clearly a transformation that will be considered significant enough to appeal to all category users. Although the graphics

changes are significant, including the bottle, label and cap color, as well as the brand name, current users are still able to find the key graphic. Were it not for that key graphic, this would have been a difficult transition; as it happened, both transitions were well executed.

A final tip is to not underestimate the intelligence of your target consumer. When it comes to remarkability, you can push them further than you think. They operate on fast impressions, and they won't take the time to analyze your selling proposition. Keep it simple, and keep it remarkable—which is not usually complicated.

Graphic Presentation

At this point, I am going to assume you are not a graphic designer. In that case, you will create a crude drawing of your graphic presentation based on the Graphic Presentation Template that follows. This is the model that I use to communicate my ideas to my design staff. It isn't pretty but I promise, it will work for you too. You are essentially creating an image to give to your graphic designer the assignment to create the layout that will communicate your selling proposition. I have used over fifty images in this book as examples to support the marketing distinctions I have shared. As you work, you will find it helpful to revisit those that address whatever issues confront you as you create your graphic presentation.

The best way to create your graphic presentation is to find a large board that you can easily erase as you refine your way to your final concept. Whatever your impact point, a homepage, a storefront, a package, a brochure, a billboard ad or anything else, you will create your graphic presentation while being mindful of how your target consumer's eyes are likely to track through it. When you sketch it out, be sure to make it very large, giving you lots of room to play with the size and location of your elements. I personally have no formal graphic design education. It is not necessary.

I have developed the following template to characterize the relative relationships among the positioning elements. This is appropriate for any graphic presentation, be it a storefront or a banner ad or anything else. You will not likely conform to it perfectly. Use it as a guide.

Focus on two aspects of your graphic presentation. First is the impact of your layout. Impact occurs when a visual component causes target consumers to engage in your selling proposition. This is likely a bold graphic that takes their eye to a key element. The eye should begin in the upper left area of the presentation, and track down through the middle to the lower right corner of the presentation. This is a general rule. You can deviate as the eye tracks but upper left to lower right is the general overall track you want.

Second is the order of importance in which your communication elements are read. Begin evaluating your communication as common sense tells you how the eye will track its way through your message. Do not force the eye to move to more than four elements. Elements are defined here as a cluster of words, or graphics with words that work as one unit when glanced at. You will remember earlier I recommended that you combine the brand/sub-brand and the generic descriptor into one element as well as the benefit and its attribute drivers. Beyond that, do not add any more information…it will only clutter your selling proposition.

The "WOW" must happen within the first two elements; consolidate your message where it makes sense. Your benefit with its two attribute drivers (as on the Sandblaster package) will function as one message. Your brand/sub-brand and your generic descriptor also function together as one message. The eye is not required to move to another area of the graphic presentation to get the complete message.

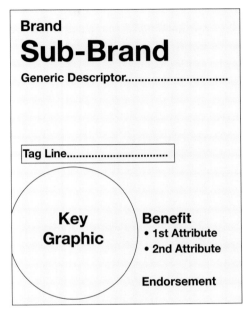

As you review the tracking of your communication, remember that you never want to force the target consumer to assemble your selling proposition. They will bail out on you in a heartbeat. You are responsible for doing that, and doing it well.

Once you have pulled it together it is time to hand it off to your graphic designer. You must remember, you are the expert in communicating your selling proposition. Your graphic designer will be skilled at interpreting your direction only if you are strictly in control providing clear direction based on the template, and all that you have learned. Most graphic designers have no formal marketing education and very few marketing skills. You will need to watch out for "pull" as your graphic designer will use all of the tricks that others have been using as well. Your final exercise will add needed impact to the graphic presentation that you and your graphic designer have developed.

Impact

FIRST: This exercise is creatively in your hands because you are intimately familiar with the characteristics of your business, and your teammates are not. You will need to take the time to create a short (three to five) list of impact options that you feel are appropriate. I suggest you go back to the impact section in Chapter 9 and review it so you are clear about what constitutes a true significant impact. If you have employees, you can ask them to create options as well. They will probably come up with a couple that you may have missed. You will have to use your knowledge of impact to evaluate their lists as they do not have the knowledge that you now enjoy. Impact is accomplished by adding a unique graphic element to your graphic presentation in such a way that it draws immediate attention. You will therefore create options using the graphic presentation you have developed and expose them to your teammates. Once you have three to five, you will send them to your teammates using the following guideline:

TEAMMATE REQUEST:

MY BUSINESS DEFINITION: (EXAMPLE; I have a video sales and rental business.)

IMPACT DEFINITION: A graphic element within my graphic presentation that draws the attention of my target consumer.

EXAMPLE: RETAIL VIDEO STORE— The bright yellow Odyssey Video building

Below are three different graphic presentations that are being considered for my business. Please rank

Your Business
(Very Brief)

1) What is your Product or Service?: _____

_____

2) Key Impact Point: _____   Secondary Impact Point:_____

3) Your Category: _____

4) Key Benefit: _____

5) Key Attributes: _____

6) Character?:   Yes _____   No _____

7) Remarkable?:   Yes _____   No _____

NOTES

_____
_____
_____
_____
_____
_____
_____
_____
_____
_____
_____
_____
_____
_____
_____
_____

Brand

Benefit

Generic
Descriptor

Key
Attributes

Benefit

Attribute
Drivers

Call To
Action

Brand

Sub-Brand

Generic
Descriptor

Key Graphic

Benefit

Attribute
Drivers

Endorsement

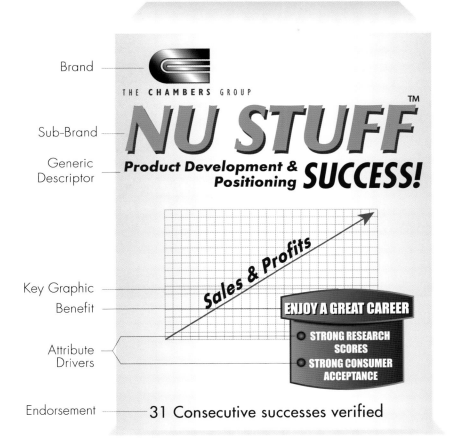

Brand   Sub-Brand

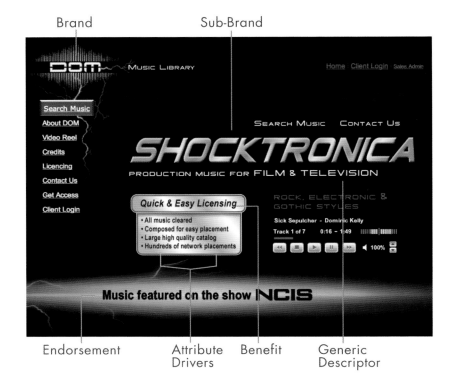

Endorsement   Attribute   Benefit   Generic
                Drivers   Descriptor

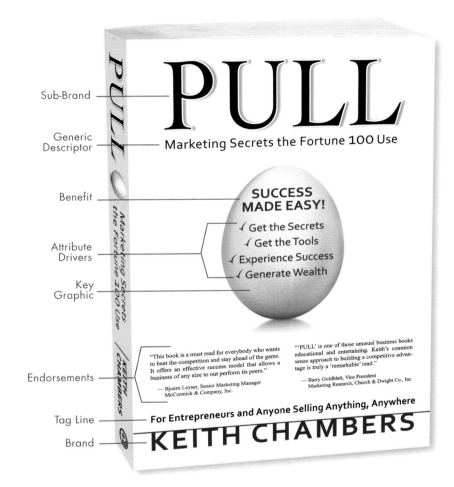

Sub-Brand

Generic Descriptor

Benefit

Attribute Drivers

Key Graphic

Endorsements

Tag Line

Brand

PULL

Marketing Secrets the Fortune 100 Use

SUCCESS MADE EASY!

✓ Get the Secrets
✓ Get the Tools
✓ Experience Success
✓ Generate Wealth

"This book is a must read for everybody who wants to beat the competition and stay ahead of the game. It offers an effective success model that allows a business of any size to out perform its peers."

— Bjoern Leyser, Senior Marketing Manager
McCormick & Company, Inc.

"'PULL' is one of those unusual business books educational and entertaining. Keith's common sense approach to building a competitive advantage is truly a 'remarkable' read."

— Barry Goldblatt, Vice President
Marketing Research, Church & Dwight Co., Inc

For Entrepreneurs and Anyone Selling Anything, Anywhere

KEITH CHAMBERS

(spine) *Marketing Secrets the Fortune 100 Use*   KEITH CHAMBERS

GLOSSARY

Appropriate: Relative to creating communication elements that are considered remarkable by target consumers. They must also be considered appropriate. Another way to say it is that they must be acceptable to the target, not offensive, irrelevant or inappropriate.

Benefit: What the target consumer gets out of using your product or service.

Brand: The name by which a product or group of products are referred.

Character: Referenced in the remarkability paradigm, it is the substance that is added to a selling proposition that target consumers will relate to. It can occur in any of the communication elements, such as the *Go-Gurt* sub-brand name or its outrageous looking illustrated skate boarding kid key graphic.

Communications Model: A document that identifies 15 specific elements that together comprise all of the elements that make up a selling proposition.

Endorsement: A favorable referral for your product or service from an outside party.

Generic Descriptor: A short statement that accurately defines your product or service. It typically follows the product name.

Graphic Presentation: A complete graphic display of your selling proposition that is encountered by your target consumer at your impact point.

Impact: A key graphic of any kind, at your impact point, that causes target consumers to engage (develop an interest) in your selling proposition.

Impact Point: The point at which your target consumer encounters your selling proposition.

Key Graphic: A strong graphic that communicates something significant about your selling proposition.

Negative Attribute: A characteristic of your product or service that needs to be communicated in order to overcome an objection that is perceived by your target consumer.

Performance Attribute: A characteristic of your product or service that defines what it does when used by the target consumer.

Physical Attribute: A physical characteristic of your product or service.

Positioning Statement: A short paragraph that characterizes your product or service and what it offers your specific target consumer.

Pull: A key distinction in the remarkability paradigm that refers to the nature of consumers to take extraordinary communication elements, and adapt to them such that they become ordinary over time.

Remarkable: The nature of a complete selling proposition that is considered extraordinary by target consumers. It typically occurs as a breakthrough within an established category.

Remarkable Triggers: The nature of a specific communication element that is considered extraordinary by target consumers. When two or three are present within a selling proposition, the selling proposition itself is considered remarkable.

Remarkability Paradigm: A series of observations that relate to each other in such a way as to accurately characterize how humans react to selling propositions.

Selling Proposition: The complete sales message for any product or service. It answers the question of why the target consumer should buy.

Sub-Brand: A secondary brand to one that is already established. It is typically more prominent than its brand as it characterizes a group of products within the brand.

Tag Line: A short group of words that highlight a specific characteristic of your product or service.

Unremarkable: The nature of any communication element that target consumers have become familiar and comfortable with.

INDEX

Appropriate 34, 42, 46, 60, 73, 74, 79, 81, 82, 83, 84, 90, 93, 97, 104, 105, 110, 111, 114, 115, 116, 131, 134, 135, 141, 148, 179, 183, 189, 198, 199, 200, 201, 202, 206, 208

Benefit 36, 59, 73, 96, 103, 109, 110, 111, 112, 113, 114, 115, 116, 117, 118, 119, 120, 121, 122, 125, 126, 127, 129, 131, 141, 151, 152, 154, 155, 156, 162, 167, 169, 180, 184, 191, 192, 193, 194, 195, 201, 207

Brand 5, 10, 11, 15, 22, 23, 36, 51, 54, 55, 56, 57, 74, 81, 83, 84, 89, 93, 94, 97, 98, 99, 100, 101, 102, 103, 104, 105, 106, 107, 108, 109, 111, 115, 116, 122, 123, 125, 127, 128, 129, 130, 132, 133, 134, 135, 137, 138, 140, 145, 150, 151, 152, 154, 155, 159, 163, 167, 169, 180, 186, 187, 188, 189, 190, 201, 205, 207

Character 20, 59, 78, 79, 80, 81, 82, 83, 87, 88, 89, 90, 96, 98, 99, 102, 130, 104, 105, 106, 115, 127, 128, 131, 132, 133, 142, 151, 155, 167, 186, 187, 188, 189, 195, 203

Communications Model 91, 92, 93, 151, 158, 180, 181, 183,

Endorsement 82, 106, 117, 130, 131, 138, 152, 167, 169, 195, 196, 218

Generic Descriptor 35, 36, 80, 95, 96, 97, 111, 127, 148, 150, 152, 154, 167, 184, 185, 186, 187, 188, 189, 201, 207

Graphic Presentation 73, 135, 147, 148, 149, 151, 154, 201, 203, 205, 206, 207, 208, 209

Impact 27, 28, 32, 33, 34, 35, 36, 45, 46, 48, 56, 59, 60, 72, 83, 90, 93, 98, 101, 119, 125, 134, 135, 136, 147, 148, 151, 154, 160, 165, 167, 200, 206, 208

Impact Point 27, 32, 33, 34, 35, 36, 45, 46, 48, 59, 72, 90, 93, 98, 125, 128, 135, 147, 148, 160, 200, 206

Key Graphic 80, 129, 131, 132, 133, 134, 142, 152, 167, 197, 198, 205

Negative Attribute 118, 124, 125, 192

Performance Attribute 36, 118, 119, 124, 125, 127

Physical Attribute 118, 119, 122, 125, 127

Positioning Statement 44, 45, 49

Pull 76, 77, 78, 90, 105, 126, 157, 165,

167, 172, 173, 174, 183, 189, 208, 209

Remarkable 28, 42, 46, 48, 49, 50, 59, 72, 73, 74, 75, 76, 77, 78, 79, 80, 81, 82, 85, 87, 88, 89, 90, 93, 96, 98, 100, 102, 110, 111, 117, 119, 120, 122, 123, 124, 125, 127, 130, 131, 133, 134, 135, 137, 138, 139, 142, 143, 144, 145, 148, 149, 153, 155, 156, 157, 158, 159, 162, 163, 165, 167, 171, 173, 177, 180, 181, 189, 199, 200, 202, 205

Remarkable Triggers 76, 78, 80, 88, 90, 93, 142, 144, 157, 159, 163, 171, 180

Remarkability Paradigm 9, 67, 91, 173, 181, 183

Selling Proposition 17, 18, 27, 28, 29, 30, 31, 32, 33, 34, 35, 36, 37, 45, 46, 48, 49, 50, 58, 72, 73, 74, 75, 76, 77, 80, 81, 83, 84, 85, 89, 90, 91, 93, 97, 98, 99, 100, 102, 109, 110, 114, 115, 116, 119, 120, 125, 126, 129, 132, 134, 135, 139, 141, 147, 148, 149, 152, 154, 155, 157, 158, 160, 161, 162, 165, 171, 177, 181, 203, 204, 205, 206, 207

Sub-Brand 80, 93, 94, 95, 105, 106, 107, 108, 109, 115, 116, 123, 152, 167, 180, 186, 187, 188, 189

Tag Line 96, 127, 128, 129, 154, 167, 194, 195

Unremarkable 42, 48, 49, 50, 71, 72, 73, 74, 75, 77, 78, 79, 82, 85, 86, 90, 98, 110, 115, 117, 118, 119, 130, 135, 142, 143, 152, 154, 159, 167, 173, 203, 209

Paradigm 9, 67, 68, 70, 71, 72, 73, 76, 77, 78, 79, 81, 82, 85, 89, 90, 91, 92, 100, 111, 120, 142, 153, 173, 181, 183, 203, 209

Research 8, 11, 13, 14, 15, 21, 41, 67, 75, 80, 101, 111, 114, 118, 122, 157, 158, 161, 162, 163, 164

Orville Redenbacher 15, 48, 54, 103

Splenda 30, 31, 32, 75, 88, 95, 105

SeaTales 44

VCR Plus 36, 37, 38, 39

Henry Yuen 35, 36

Gemstar 35, 37, 38, 39

JumpStart 47

Go-Gurt 54, 80, 81, 105, 106, 144

Ivory Snow 83, 84

Milk 'n Cereal Bars 96

Van de Kamp's 103, 104

SandBlaster 44, 107, 120, 121, 136, 207

Nu Stuff 69, 177

Shocktronica 150, 151, 177

Pull 76, 77, 78, 90, 105, 126, 157, 165, 167, 172, 173, 174, 183, 189, 208, 209

Team 14, 22, 23, 25, 41, 47, 49, 64, 65, 67, 69, 74, 79, 82, 83, 103, 104, 116, 122, 123, 128, 147, 179, 181, 183, 184, 185, 186, 188, 203

Awareness 6, 8, 33, 53, 60, 61, 62, 67, 78, 99, 108, 114, 115, 123, 128, 132, 136, 171, 173, 174, 181

Platform 10

Risk 21, 50, 89, 173, 203, 204

About the Author

"Free enterprise is basically war," says Keith Chambers, founder and president of The Chambers Group. "If you are among those who don't believe this, you are likely to become one of its casualties." Keith's innovative techniques and successes have kept his clients from becoming casualties for over thirty years and have made him one of the nation's leading marketing consultants for Fortune 100 brands.

Keith has assisted more than five hundred goods and service providers in formulating their marketing messages, including *Arm & Hammer*, *Stagg*, *Coppertone*, *Claritin*, *Crest Spinbrush*, *First Response*, *Trojan*, *Scotch-Brite 3M*, Miss America, and *McCormick*.

Graduating from the Arizona State University with an undergraduate degree in Advertising and Marketing, Keith established The Chambers Group in 1976. The firm began as a successful package design studio for brands such as *Hi-C, Van de Kamps, Hunts, MJB*, and *Minute Maid*. It soon became clear, though, that his clients needed more than dynamic packaging; they required a comprehensive and cohesive marketing strategy. The Chambers Group expanded its services to include naming and positioning.

A turning point came in 1988, when *Sega* approached him for assistance with their package design image for a new high-powered home video game platform. When told the company had yet to name their product, Keith saw an opportunity. His group created the brand *Sega Genesis*; by its second year, *Sega Genesis* was exceeding $500 million in sales. Instantly, The Chambers Group redefined itself into a unique creative marketing company, helping clients to fully develop the branding and positioning of their products.

Considered unorthodox by many, The Chambers Group brought originality to their marketing approach. "In the old days, a client would tell us what he wanted," Keith explains. "Today, they share what they need and we fulfill it." The relationship with the consumer has changed, as well. Rather than develop a marketing concept and then measure the consumer response to it, Keith consults the consumer first to define their needs, ensuring they are met in the new concept.

Keith brings innovation and fierce loyalty to each of his clients, ensuring they are able to survive the constantly changing battlefield of the marketplace. "If you are part of the change, you'll be successful. Bystanders will get their butts kicked sooner or later." His best inspiration is the fear of failure. "Every problem has a solution, especially in marketing," Keith says.

The Chambers Group is headquartered in Los Angeles and has offices in Dallas and Philadelphia. Keith's proudest achievement, though, is his relationship with his sons, Branden and Eric. Together, they have established Chambers Brothers Entertainment, which has developed a long list of shows, including Spike TV's *Ultimate Gamer*, and is currently in production on the first of two feature films, *Cheech and Chong's Smokin' Animated Movie*.

Keith has begun work on his next book and looks forward to the day when he can conduct business from his surfboard.